Faithful Neighbors

Faithful Neighbors

CHRISTIAN-MUSLIM VISION & PRACTICE

Edited by

ROBERT S. HEANEY,

ZEYNEB SAYILGAN,

AND CLAIRE HAYMES

Morehouse Publishing
NEW YORK

Unless otherwise noted, the Scripture quotations contained herein are
from the New Revised Standard Version Bible, copyright © 1989 by the
Division of Christian Education of the National Council of Churches
of Christ in the U.S.A. Used by permission. All rights reserved.

Morehouse Publishing, 19 East 34th Street, New York, NY 10016

Morehouse Publishing is an imprint of Church Publishing Incorporated.
www.churchpublishing.org

Cover design by Jennifer Kopec, 2Pug Design
Typeset by John Turnbull

Library of Congress Cataloging-in-Publication Data
Heaney, Robert Stewart, 1972- editor.
Faithful neighbors:
Christian-Muslim vision and practice /
edited by Robert S. Heaney, Zeyneb Sayilgan, and Claire Haymes.
Includes bibliographical references.
LCCN 2016018205 (print) | LCCN 2016011281 (ebook) |
ISBN 9780819232564 (ebook) | ISBN 9780819232557 (pbk.)
Islam—Relations—Anglican Communion. | Anglican
Communion—Relations—Islam. | Islam—Relations—Christianity. |
Christianity and other religions—Islam.
BP172.5.a6 (print) |
BP172.5.A6 F35 2016 (ebook) |
261.2/7—dc23
LC record available at https://lccn.loc.gov/2016018205

Printed in the United States of America

CONTENTS

FOREWORD

Of the many challenges that face this world, living with religious diversity remains an acute issue. Globalization has led to the vast movement of people, such that most countries are religiously diverse. Yet tensions and suspicions abound. We are not good at living together in constructive ways.

It is fairly easy to find a book that explains the beliefs and practices of each religion. You can learn what your neighbor believes by sitting in a good library or by downloading a book on your e-book reader. It is also fairly easy to find countless books on interfaith and interreligious theory—how conceptually one might think about the engagement with the other. But what is hard to find is a good book that actually takes the reader inside different encounters across religions, from friendship to conferences. This is the achievement of this remarkable book.

Robert Heaney in his opening chapter muses on the dangers of "yacht dialogue." This is when liberal advocates of the different traditions come together to float increasingly adrift from the communities they represent. They are professional dialogue participants, who are often very critical of their coreligionists who are conservative or orthodox. Heaney insists, rightly, that this mode of dialogue is deeply problematic. If the challenge is living with religious diversity, then the solution is not to disparage those who are most committed in your community.

Zeyneb Sayilgan starts in a really interesting place. How can a Muslim committed to the truth of her religion support and affirm the appropriateness of dialogue and friendships across the religious divide? Her answer is a careful exegesis of the Qur'an. She is being faithful to the text that she believes is the very word of God. There are, she argues, solid Qur'anic reasons for participation in interfaith dialogue.

The stage is set. The subsequent chapters dig down. Building on substantial data, we learn how and when congregations participate in interfaith conversation. Often the chapters are biographical; they tell stories of a journey in life toward greater connectivity and affection. They describe projects realized, mutual understandings attained, and constructive options explored. They are deeply hopeful narratives.

The challenge of religious diversity is not going to be solved by liberals from each tradition climbing on a yacht and sailing away, nor is the solution increasing retrenchment, misunderstanding, and crude caricatures. Instead Heaney and Sayilgan document in the concluding chapter the seven aspects that make up constructive interfaith conversations. These aspects capture the necessity for authenticity and connection within a framework that recognizes and admits difference and the inevitable differences in power relations.

This is a book that has potential to be life-changing. With valuable study questions, it can take a congregation to a new place—a place where we all start becoming part of the solution to religious diversity rather than part of the problem.

IAN S. MARKHAM

ACKNOWLEDGMENTS

It is a delight to come together as God's people. This delight was in many ways the reason we joined together to produce this volume. Gathering with sisters and brothers, of our own faith or another, is something we wanted to reflect on and to encourage others to do. We hope to have demystified to some degree the process by which believers can come together for mutual encouragement. It is an ordinary act with extraordinary power to transform.

In that spirit we wish to thank the generative community for this book, which includes participants in conferences in Alexandria, Virginia, and in Dodoma, Tanzania. Therefore, we thank Archbishop Jacob Chimeledya, archbishop of Tanzania; Sheikh Mustapha, sheikh of Dodoma region; Dr. Joshua Rutere; the Rev. Canon Moses Matonya; Waziri Ally; the Rev. Chris Ahrends; the Rt. Rev. Johannes Otieno Angela; Mohammed Aogo; the Rev. Joel O. Atong; the Rt. Rev. Philip D. Baji; the Rev. Patrick M. Bendera; Shamim Daudi; the Rev. Peter Gachira; the Rt. Rev. Given M. Gaula; the Rev. Elkana Gonda; Sheikh Mikdad Halfani; Athmann Hotty; Dr. Ziddy Haji Issa; the Rev. Hilda Kabia; the Rev. Fr. Martin Bob Kalimbe; Musa Mwale Kanenje; Professor Assad Kipanga; Sheikh Aly Juma Liwuchu; the Rev. George Otieno Lawi; the Rev. Caleb Loan; the Rev. Emmanuel Madinda; the Rev. George Omondi Markoyath;

the Rev. Lusungu Benja Mbilinyi; Musa Ogera Mbuya; the Rev. David M. Mdabuko; Sheikh Juma Mussa Mhina; Sheikh Juma Rashid Mhina; Ashura Mhoji; Professor Canon Wilfred Mlay; the Rev. Peter Mkengi; the Rev. Canon Yusufu Mkunda; the Rt. Rev. William F. Mndolwa; the Rt. Rev. Gerard E. Mpango; Sheikh Msaga; Venerable Father Justice Moses Msini; the Rev. Canon Ajabu Mtweve; the Rev. Canon Phanuel Mung'ong'o; Mtaima Ally Mustapha; Dr. Esha Faki Mwinyihaji; Asenath Mwithigah; the Rev. Isaac Odhiambo Arika; the Rev. Dr. George M. Okoth; Abdallah Omari; the Rev. Mary Ong'injo; Rashid Owino; Sheikh Haji Rashid; Sheikh Ahmed Saidi; Abtwalibu Salimu; the Rev. Nuhu Sallanya; Salih Sayilgan; the Rev. Chediel Elinaza Sendoro; Cecil Simbaulanga; Sheilla Sitande; Elisha Sudhe; the Rt. Rev. Samuel Sudhe; Sheikh Mohammed Swalehe; Sheikh Abdulla Talib; Abdalah Ramadhan Ukwaju; Shaban Yusuf; the Rev. Leslie Steffensen; Sister Munira Salim-Mohamed Abdalla; the Rev. Randy Alexander; the Very Rev. Collins E. Asonye; the Rev. Jo Belser; the Rev. Dr. Susan Fellows; the Rev. Dr. David T. Gortner; Hakan Gülerce; Taalibah Hassan; Brad Linboom; Kyle Martindale; Jonathan Musser; Marie Monsen; Molly O'Brien; Fatimah Popal; the Rev. Gay Rahn; Dr. Safiya Samman; Talib Shareef; Brandon Turner; Hartley Hobson Wensing; and Katherine Wood.

James Stambaugh, Postulant for Holy Orders from the Diocese of the Rio Grande, and member of the Center for Anglican Communion Studies team, worked on additional resource gathering. We are grateful to him and also to Dr. Lucinda Mosher, the Rev. Dr. David Marshall, and the Rev. Dr. Richard Sudworth for suggesting additional interfaith resources.

We are indebted to the Henry Luce Foundation for their generous funding for interfaith work at Virginia Theological Seminary over six years. Their grants allowed for an expectation, and thus culture of, conversation, reconciliation, dialogue, and exploration that continues beyond the end of the funding period. We thank the Rev. Dr. Barney Hawkins for his work with Katherine Wood during the first year of the grant. Special thanks are due to Nancy Bryan, Editor Director of Church Publishing. Her commitment and vision for this project played a decisive part in making this publication possible.

This volume is an expression of just one aspect of the work we do in the Center for Anglican Communion Studies, Virginia Theological Seminary. The Center is grateful to all who contributed to this work as authors and as conversation partners. We are part of and we are made by the communities we come from. The leadership and collegiality of Virginia Theological Seminary make the Center for Anglican Communion Studies and its work possible. We are grateful for the significant contributions to interfaith conversation that the Very Rev. Dr. Ian S. Markham, the dean and president of vts, makes. We are grateful that he has supported this project from the beginning and has agreed to write the foreword to this volume. It is our prayer that the research, the testimonies and the theologizing in this volume will encourage readers to explore what it means to be faithful neighbors.

ROBERT S. HEANEY
ZEYNEB SAYILGAN
CLAIRE HAYMES

THE Center
for Anglican
Communion Studies

VISION OF THE CENTER
FOR ANGLICAN COMMUNION STUDIES

This collection of essays emerges from work carried out under the auspices of Virginia Theological Seminary's Center for Anglican Communion Studies. The vision of the Center is often summed up in the words "promoting and practicing better community for the Communion." The Communion spans 165 countries and includes some eighty-five million Christian believers. It is deeply intercultural and interreligious and, if Anglicans are going to practice better community, then they must continue to listen and learn across cultures and across religions.

To that end, three imperatives direct the work of the Center: reflect, resource, reconcile. To *reflect* together is to host conversations, consultations, and conferences both at Virginia Seminary and beyond. Reflection is to strive to listen deeply not only to the voice of sisters and brothers but to be open to the voice of God in such encounters. To *resource* Anglicans and their faithful neighbors means producing reports, videos, and other publications that help contribute to a common vision and the common good as shaped by theological commitments. To *reconcile* is to be committed to peace, to work toward effective understandings of peace building, and to work toward deeper understandings and appreciation across sectional, cultural, and religious divisions.

Part One

FAITHFUL NEIGHBORS: THEOLOGICAL RATIONALE

1

A CHRISTIAN RATIONALE
FOR INTERFAITH ENGAGEMENT
~

Robert S. Heaney

"Yacht dialogue" is the term coined to describe interfaith conversation that drifts ever peacefully and ever further from the mainland of faith commitment and faith communities. Very nice and polite people from different faith perspectives come on board to meet together, talk together, eat together, and produce beautiful statements of intent together. Like vacationers they enjoy each other's company, all the while drifting from the moorings of their communities and their faith. The deck sparkles as common understandings and common vision are built on apparently objective and universal principles independent of the faith of the constituencies they purport to represent. This is a caricature, of course, but one that is, unfortunately, not altogether unfamiliar.

The commitment of the staff, both Muslim and Christian, at Virginia Theological Seminary's Center for Anglican Communion Studies is to engage in interfaith conversation and interfaith vision not on the basis of the lowest common denominator of inoffensive niceness. Our work together is not based on nor does it seek reductionism or demythologization. Rather, we work together in a spirit of respect for our traditions, in good faith (orthodoxy), and toward right practice (orthopraxis) within and between our traditions. To enter into conversation and common vision is not expected to dilute or deny one's faith. Rather, because we are people of faith we enter into relationship, conversation, and common vision. To speak of the other is not then to define one's self over against another or to deny the common humanity that we share. Rather, it is to respect differences, for we understand that difference is not simply what separates us but is also what makes us present to each other. To enter into conversation and search for common vision is work that is moored close to faith commitments and faith communities. It is anchored in the tradition.

I would argue, from a Christian perspective, that these conversations and any common vision that emerges will be understood in reference to that theological and practical category seemingly celebrated and shunned in equal measure: mission. This chapter outlines a Christian understanding of mission and then clarifies how a vision and practice of interfaith cooperation can be nourished by an emerging theology of mission.

THE ALMOST COMPREHENSIVE LIST

According to the monotheistic faiths, God is One. Indeed, for followers of Jesus the oneness of God is the greatest commandment. "The first [commandment] is, 'Hear, O Israel: the Lord our God, the Lord is one; you shall love the Lord your God with all your heart, and with all your soul, and with all your mind, and with all your strength'" (Mark 12:29–30). As Christians we "stand under Moses' authority, under the teaching of the apostle to the gentiles, under the gracious yoke of Jesus

Christ. . . .[We] hearken to this commandment. The Lord our God is One."[1] Of course, the oneness of God cannot be reduced to the idea of one. That is to say, monotheism recognizes that applying math to God is not straightforward. Miroslav Volf illustrates the problem through an example provided by Denys Turner and that I call "the almost comprehensive list."[2] Imagine you had the capacity to count the total number of things that have existed, do exist, and will exist. Imagine presenting this list to your friends. A rather shy companion interrupts the mood, "Excuse me. I see that your list is truly impressive. However, haven't you forgotten something?"

"Surely not," you respond.

"Well," your friend continues, "I'm afraid you've left God off your list."

What an omission! You now realize that your list is neither comprehensive nor complete but is an almost comprehensive list. The very one who made everything on the list and made everything possible on the list is not on the list. But, would simply adding a "+1" to the list redress the problem? It would not.

"God is not one thing among many other things in the universe, not even one supremely important thing without which none of the other things could exist. Instead, God is unique and categorically different from the world."[3] In short, the almost comprehensible list needs to remain so. For applying math to God is not the same as applying math to the vast array of creatures in the world. One God and one tree are not equivalent uses of oneness. Applying math to divinity is a tricky business. Math might, in some parallel universe, comprehend all that exists. But math cannot comprehend God. However, while math cannot comprehend God it can, Volf reminds us, counteract incorrect beliefs about God.[4]

While God cannot be reduced to human counting, certain things can be deduced from human counting. For example, to say that there is one undivided divine essence discounts there being a pantheon of gods. At the same time, this statement also discounts the notion that the one god is in the same category as the gods belonging to the pantheon if these gods did exist. Even equating God with this imaginary oneness where the one could be joined by other ones is a reductionist view of God. It would be, as Volf reminds us, idolatry. [5] It might be suspected that even the most ardent monotheist is tempted by such idolatry. Certainly, this is the witness of the Jewish, Muslim, and Christian scriptures:

> Those who worship vain idols
> forsake their true loyalty. (Jon. 2:8)

> What use is an idol
> once its maker has shaped it—
> a cast image, a teacher of lies?
> For its maker trusts in what has been made,
> though the product is only an idol that cannot
>   speak! (Hab. 2:18)

> For all the gods of the peoples are idols,
> But the LORD made the heavens. (1 Chron. 16:26;
>   see Ps. 96:5)

> I am the LORD, that is my name;
> my glory I give to no other,
> nor my praise to idols. (Isa. 42:8)

> . . . my dear friends, flee from the worship of idols.
>   (1 Cor. 10:14)

> You know that when you were pagans, you were
> enticed and led astray to idols that could not speak.
> (1 Cor. 12:2)

For the people of those regions report about us what kind of welcome we had among you, and how you turned to God from idols, to serve a living and true God. (1 Thess. 1:9)

Little children, keep yourselves from idols. (1 John 5:21)

There is no god but God. (Qur'an 47:19)

Say, "God is one and only." (Qur'an 112:1)

And do not argue with the People of the Scripture except in a way that is best, except for those who commit injustice among them, and say, "We believe in that which has been revealed to us and revealed to you. And our God and your God is one." (Qur'an 29:46)

Say: "O People of the Book! Come to common terms as between us and you: that we worship none but God; that we associate no partners with him; that we erect not, from among ourselves, Lords and patrons other than God." (Qur'an 3:64)[6]

Whatever oneness means it cannot reduce God to one of a category that others belong to, may belong to, or may be imagined to belong to. For if oneness did mean this then monotheists, of all traditions, would be guilty of idolatry.[7] Formally we say that God is in a distinct ontological category. In other words, God is the Creator, all else is creation. In short, the oneness of God is a complex matter.

If the oneness of God is difficult to comprehend, then applying threeness to God will also be difficult. As every Christian preacher and teacher knows as Trinity Sunday approaches, this is indeed the case. As has often been said, Trinity Sunday is the high feast of heresy and idolatry for the church. In countless churches throughout the world, the threeness of God is counted as water, steam, and ice; as a three-leafed shamrock; or, as shell, yolk, and white. The creator is reduced to creation and is reduced to human counting. Yet, if the oneness of God is unique then it should also be expected that the threeness of God will be unique in a way that water, shamrocks, and eggs are not. If the oneness of God cannot be reduced to human counting, so too the threeness of God cannot be reduced to human counting. Christians, Jews, and Muslims are in agreement. The divine essence cannot be divided. Indeed, it may be that what the Prophet Muhammad condemned is something that Christian leaders would also want to reject. The Qur'an states: "They do blaspheme who say: God is one of three in a Trinity: for there is no god except One God. If they desist not from their word [of blasphemy], verily a grievous penalty will befall the blasphemers among them" (5:73). Trinitarian monotheists agree with the word of the Qur'an on this point. God is not one of three in a Trinity. For to divide the divine essence into three gods of limited power is polytheism.[8] Again, Volf is helpful:

> There are *no* individual essences *in* God. Instead, to say that there are three "Persons" in God means only that there are three eternal, inseparable, and interpenetrating agencies; in each, the other two are present, and in each, the single divine essence is present.[9]

The Mission of God

I will not presume to explain the Trinity, any more than I will presume to explain the oneness of God. Rather, in light of the mysterious revelation of the oneness of the one God comes the revelation that this God is the source of life and is at work in and through creation. This divine nature, revelation, and work Christians associate with the *missio Dei* (the mission of God). *Mission* is a term in Christian thought that first and foremost refers to the nature of God. We often understand it to refer to activity of the church but it is first and foremost a divine referent. For Christians, God is one. But, God is not an individual.[10] In the very heart of God there is complexity, community, relationship. God is sentness. God is overflowing life and love and grace. God is the boundary-crossing God. This boundary crossing is seen both within the heart of God (the immanent Trinity) and is seen in the first missional act: "let there be light."

The Edinburgh missionary conference of 1910 brought together 1,200 participants representing 160 mission boards or societies. The goal was to develop strategies for the speedy completion of world evangelization. It could be done. It would be done. Christianity would expand from the so-called civilized centers of Europe and North America out into the so-called pagan and uncivilized corners of the world. It was an anthropocentric or ecclesiocentric time, and this model for mission was soon challenged by the devastating effects of a world war and the devastating potential of another world war. In place of a rationalist optimism, a more circumspect theologizing that faced up to the failings of humanity and Western Christian expansionism was needed. One year before Hitler came to power, Karl Barth called the church back to its Trinitarian source:

> Must not even the most faithful missionary, the most convinced friend of missions, have reason to reflect that the term *missio* was in the ancient Church an expression of the doctrine of the Trinity—namely the expression of the divine sending forth of self, the sending of the Son and Holy Spirit?[11]

A Christian theology of mission does not belong in the chapter "What is the church?" It belongs in the chapter "Who is God?"

Given that mission is first understood to refer to the nature of God, how might this begin to affect how Christians understand, discern, and participate in God's mission? At least three things are apposite particularly in relation to interfaith conversation. First, mission is who God is. Mission is God's creative act. If Christians can talk of the mission of believers or of the church it is two steps removed from the divine referent. The Christian vocation is to discern God's mission and seek to participate in God's mission. The agent of mission is not, therefore, human; it is divine. The temptation for Christians to displace the sovereignty of God in favor of a bloated sense of human agency is ever with us. It is a temptation to which Christians succumb all too often in religious and mission history. Taking heed of God's mission may well begin more with contemplation and discernment than it does with strategies, priorities, or budgets. Participation in God's mission emerges from deeper knowledge and experience of God. Mission begins with the breath of God. Mission is entered into through the breath of prayer. It is entered into by coming together to ask for God's mercy and God's guidance.

Second, because of the otherness and sovereignty of God and the ongoing temptation of human pride, Christians are called to listen intently not only for the voice of God's grace but also to listen intently for the voice of God's judgment. That means a deep listening to the "otherness" of Scripture and of the testimony of faithful forebears. It also means, because of who God is, a deep listening to the "otherness of others" across cultures, traditions, and religions. Arguably, the best theology is done across cultural and religious boundaries. Indeed, the Christian vision of the end times testifies to a divinely re-created city where the wisdom of the world will be gathered:

> I saw no temple in the city, for its temple is the
> Lord God the Almighty and the Lamb. And the city
> has no need of sun or moon to shine on it, for the
> glory of God is its light, and its lamp is the Lamb.
> The nations will walk by its light, and the kings of
> the earth will bring their glory into it. Its gates will
> never be shut by day—and there will be no night
> there. People will bring into it the glory and the
> honor of the nations. (Rev. 21:22–26)

God's intent is to reconcile all creation to God's self. We step into the divine current when we work for and in a spirit of mutual understanding, peace, and co-operation.

Third, Christians testify to the centrality of Jesus Christ in the mission of God. God has come to the world in the person and work of Jesus Christ. Incarnating the mission of God in the life of Jesus did not come through practices of domination or proselytism. The mission of God in Christ came in service of others. The community of Jesus is still called to service of others: "[T]he greatest among you must become like the youngest, and the leader like the one who serves. . . . I am among you as one who serves" (Luke 22:26–27). As Christians we would do well to think further on how interfaith conversation and co-operation, in light of the example of Jesus, is service to others and, because of that, service to God. How, in interfaith conversation, can Christians work toward serving Muslims and Muslims work toward serving Christians? Further, we do well to recognize and remember that the Christian Gospel itself is "interconnected and mutually dependent"[12] on the traditions of other faiths and embedded in interreligious milieus in both historical and contemporary contexts.

WE CANNOT SAVE OURSELVES

If, in an iteration of Christian theology, God is mission and the first missional act is God's creation, then the second missional act is re-creation. Despite human sin, the overflowing love, grace, and life of God does not stop. It becomes expressed not just in creative action but in divine re-creative action. For Christians, that divine re-creative intent is embodied in Jesus and that can be understood as work toward renewing the ecologies of God's people and God's world. This is a re-creation that breaks out into the world through the power of God's Spirit in resurrection. Thus, Christians believe fellowship with Christ is participation in a renewed humanity.[13] The church has understood that participation in different ways. For Episcopalians and Anglicans we have identified "Five Marks of Mission." These marks can be summarized as *proclamation* of the kingdom, *formation* of disciples, *service* of those in need, work for *justice*, and attention to *ecology*. Each of these marks can inform and nourish a Christian rationale for engaging the other.

The first mark is the defining and distinctive mark of Christian mission. Christians are called in word and deed to proclaim that God's word to God's world is peace. It is mercy. It is good news. Christian proclamation of the good news of Jesus is not simply proclamation about what Jesus taught but it is also proclamation of who Jesus is. Christian Scripture, historic creeds, and historical interpretations include the fraught work of relating divinity to the person of Jesus of Nazareth. There are a wide variety of christological expressions within Christian traditions, and the conversation continues. Christians and Muslims will not reach agreement on the nature of Jesus. Nonetheless, I would argue that interreligious work predicated upon Christian demythologizing or reductionism does not serve Christian and Muslim communities, histories, and present realities well. Dialogic integrity means a recognition that Christians do indeed understand monotheism to include the proclamation of the lordship of Jesus Christ as "the only begotten Son of God" and "consubstantial to the Father" who "for us and for our salvation came down from heaven and was made incarnate by the Holy Spirit." What that proclamation means and its significance for Christians is part of the work of faithful neighbors.

While Christian proclamation of good news is not simply proclamation of the teaching of Jesus, it is not less than this. Jesus taught that the one God loves the world and that God calls us to love our neighbors (Matt. 22:34–40). The call to love God, to love neighbor, and to ground that love in word and deed is common to both Islam and Christianity. The first mark of mission then, grounded on a vision of the sovereignty and agency of God, is not justification for proselytism (the striving of human agency toward making others submit to my understanding and practice of faith). It is, rather, an invitation to testify to why the teaching and work of Jesus is good news. It is an invitation to tell the stories of how Christ has transformed lives. "So let our differences not cause hatred and strife between us. Let us vie with each other only in righteousness and good works."[14]

The remaining four marks of mission are inspired by the person and work of Jesus. Indeed, properly understood, these marks of mission emerge from how Christians understand the person and message of Jesus. Yet, given the sovereignty and agency of God, the pluralism and interconnectedness of our traditions, and the common challenges that all humans are facing, visions and practices of formation, service, justice, and ecology cannot be done in isolation. There is much we can learn from each other, there are many opportunities to spur each other on to deeper works of mercy, and there is much that we can do together. At the heart of practices of formation is the admission that we cannot save ourselves and that we are dependent on the mercy of God. But prayers are not enough. As faithful neighbors we are called to service. Prayers "must be accompanied by generosity and self-sacrifice. . . .Without giving the neighbour what we ourselves love, we do not truly love God or the neighbour."[15] As the apostolic witness to "remember the poor" (Gal. 2:10) remains, so too the Qur'an teaches, "You will not attain unto righteousness until you expend out of that which you love" (3:92). Acts of mercy independent of work to replace unjust structures and embedded practices of injustice will have limited impact. *A Common Word* states, "Muslims and Christians together make up well over half of the world's population. Without peace and justice between these two religious communities, there can be no meaningful peace in the world. The future of the world depends on peace between Muslims and Christians."[16] Practices of peace at local as well as national and international levels are part of what we are concerned with as faithful neighbors. Such practices, in the wake of diminishing resources and climate change, cannot be isolated from our identity as children of the earth.

GOD'S MISSION AND INTERFAITH ENGAGEMENT

Four things have been said at this juncture. Christians and Muslims are committed to the oneness of God. A stress on the sovereignty of God prevents inflated notions of human agency. Mission is who God is, and God is the agent of mission. Given this divine nature and divine work, believers seek to take heed of God's intent not least through five marks of mission. To conclude, and arising from such missional theologizing, I contend that unveiling idolatry, depending on God's agency, and searching for reconciliation might be useful ways to summarize a Christian rationale for engaging in interfaith conversation and cooperation.

Engaging the other means an unveiling of idolatry. In the

Christian-Muslim conversation, as we have seen, this is particularly pertinent as time and again the Qur'an challenges Christians not to confuse creatures with the creator. As Christians
this means opening ourselves up not only to the voice of God's
grace and mercy in conversation but also being open to the
voice of God's judgment in interfaith conversation. For example, my experience in leading Christian seminary students on
study tours hosted by Muslim partners is that often they come
home determined to clarify their "God talk" and their "Trinity
talk," for they often realize that simplistic doctrines of God are
incomplete or unhelpful for living in multireligious contexts.
Indeed, oversimplified and overstated visions of God can stand
in the place of the revelation of God's self. They can become
idols. Dialogue will always have, therefore, a prophetic dimension—a call away from human constructions and a call back
to the living God. Dialogue is "attentive listening, conversation
skills, empathy, study, respect," yet it is also prophetic when it
"demands honesty, conviction, courage and faith."[17] This will
mean that interfaith conversation will need to be done in a context of prayer. Our sharing together, our being together, and
our working together is dependent on God. Thus it is important that we conduct our conversations as they emerge from
practices and attitudes of prayer. Practically, this means setting places and times aside for prayer, witnessing each other
pray, sharing our prayer exercises and disciplines, and calling
on God's help for our common work. It is telling each other
stories about God's hand in our journeys and how we have experienced God's mercy at work in our lives in our communities.
At a conference that gathered individuals from a variety of faith
traditions, I asked every participant to bring with them an artifact that said something about their journey in life and faith. As
people brought pictures of loved ones and loved places, fabric
from far-off places and even a rubber duck, time and again we

heard testimony of the agency of God at work in lives and in a troubled world.

Engaging the other depends on God's agency. A stress on God's agency in God's mission will result in a contemplative, critical, and contextual approach to engaging with the world. I have emphasized the importance of prayer and hearing God's judgment on the unveiling of idolatry. Presently, I will associate the contextual task with the stress on God's agency. Simply stated, contextualization is thinking about and acting out one's faith aware of the needs and cultural patterns at work in one's context. Culture and gospel continue to emerge, hybridize, contextualize, adopt, and adapt. Indeed, there is a long history of Christian theologians engaging with, adopting, and adapting the thought and practice of the other. Jesus himself was surprised by the faith of those outside his tradition (Luke 7:9); Augustine used Neoplatonism; Aquinas accesses the Islamic rediscovery of Aristotle; modern theologians and missionaries engage with African traditional religions, existentialism, postmodernism, and postcolonialism.[18] Arguably, the reason for this engagement with the other is the belief that the primary agent in history is the God of revelation and not human beings. Thus, John S. Mbiti observes that missionaries did not bring God to Africa. God was already present and at work in Africa especially in and through African traditional religions.[19] Given such history, Ian Markham is correct: "It is indefensible to insist that a tradition that has come to us shaped by non-Christian sources should now be fossilized."[20] We have much to learn from our multireligious contexts. But this is not because we are great learners nor is it because it will make us great people (though I would not want to necessarily deny that). We have much to learn because God is ahead of us already at work in the cultures and religions of God's world.

Engaging the other is a search for reconciliation. Famously, Hans Küng observed that there will be no peace among the nations until there is peace among the religions.[21] The Christian gospel can be expressed in terms of God's work of reconciliation and the Christian vocation of reconciling. Reconciliation heals the wounds of history. Reconciliation celebrates diversity. Reconciliation builds cultures of peace.[22] As people of faith we are people of peace. While such a message gets distorted it is at the heart of the Muslim and Christian message to the world. God's intent is for peace. God's intent is for reconciliation.

Reconciliation might be thought of as operating in four areas of human life. All of these levels have an interfaith dimension and none of these areas is hermetically sealed from one another.[23] Personal reconciliation relates especially to those who have suffered violence by individuals, groups, or structures. Cultural reconciliation is needed when voices are marginalized. Political reconciliation is needed when peoples, communities, and nations are in conflict or human flourishing continues to be curtailed because of past conflict. Religious reconciliation is needed because issues such as race, gender, sexuality, proselytism, and religious violence have wounded humans and human societies. Indeed, they have threatened to tear communities apart.

Reconciliation is not predicated upon agreement or proselytism. It is predicated upon forgiveness, community, and healthy disagreement. It is a vocation.[24] For this reason not only are conversation and vision important, but joint action is also important. As people of faith face the consequences of faithlessness we can act together for the common good theologically, liturgically, socially, politically, and ecologically.[25]

Questions for Discussion

1. What artifact would you bring to an interfaith gathering that would say something about an important moment in your faith journey?

2. The Five Marks of Mission are an Anglican way of summing up the call of God to the lives of believers. How would you sum up your duty to the world as a person of faith?

3. In your experience and in your context, what situation is in particular need of practices of reconciliation? How can interfaith witness help with that need?

Notes

1. Katherine Sonderegger, *Systematic Theology,* vol. 1: *The Doctrine of God* (Minneapolis: Fortress Press, 2015), 4.

2. Miroslav Volf, *Allah: A Christian Response* (New York: Harper-Collins, 2011), 140–41.

3. Ibid., 141.

4. Ibid.

5. Ibid.

6. See www.acommonword.com.

7. Volf, *Allah,* 141.

8. Ibid., 131–35.

9. Ibid., 141–42.

10. Rowan Williams, *Arius: Heresy and Tradition,* rev. ed. (1987; Grand Rapids: Eerdmans, 2001), 266–67.

11. See Norman E. Thomas, ed., *Classic Texts in Mission and World Christianity* (Maryknoll, NY: Orbis, 1995), 105–6.

12. Ian S. Markham, *A Theology of Engagement* (Malden, MA: Blackwell, 2003), 191.

13. David J. Bosch, *Transforming Mission: Paradigm Shifts in Theology of Mission* (Maryknoll, NY: Orbis, 1991), 519.

14. *A Common Word between Us and You,* five-year anniversary ed. (Amman, Jordan: Royal Aal Al-Bayt Institute for Islamic Thought, 2012), 73.

15. Ibid., 66–67.

16. Ibid., 53.

17. Stephen B. Bevans and Roger P. Schroeder, *Constants in Context: A Theology of Mission for Today* (Maryknoll, NY: Orbis, 2004), 384.

18. See Markham, *Theology of Engagement*, 9.

19. See Robert S. Heaney, *From Historical to Critical Post-colonial Theology: The Contribution of John S. Mbiti and Jesse N. K. Mugambi* (Eugene, OR: Pickwick Publications, 2015), 94–125.

20. Ibid.

21. Hans Küng, *Global Responsibility: In Search of a New World Ethic*, trans. John Bowden (London: SCM, 1991).

22. From the mission statement of the Coventry Cross of Nails community. See Phil Groves and Angharad Parry Jones, *Living Reconciliation* (Cincinnati: Forward Movement, 2014), 16.

23. See Bevans and Schroeder, *Constants in Context*, 389–95.

24. Groves and Jones, *Living Reconciliation*, 350–61.

25. Bevans and Schroeder, *Constants in Context*, 383–84.

2

A MUSLIM RATIONALE FOR
INTERFAITH ENGAGEMENT
∼

Zeyneb Sayilgan

The latest Pew survey conducted in 2013 on the world's Muslims finds that the overwhelming majority believes that Islam is the only true religion leading to eternal salvation.[1] This is hardly surprising. Since its inception Islam has asserted itself as the final and universal faith. It confirmed previous revelations while equally offering its own unique voice. It intended to clarify and correct theological positions or practices held by various religious communities—most notably Judaism and Christianity. While it is true that a marginal but vocal minority of Muslims have taken the understanding of Islam's finality as justification to treat non-Muslims with contempt and even to harm their lives and properties, the indisputable fact is that mainstream Muslims—Sunnis and Shiites alike—have not internalized such a hostile worldview. They have often managed to live affably with people of all faiths during the course of history and in varied geographic contexts.

The Qur'an, considered to be the "Word of God" (Arabic: *kalāmullah*), has been the main channel through which this dual attitude—embrace and rejection of the "Other"—has been derived throughout Islamic history. The Scripture's relationship with other religious communities is not a straightforward or clear-cut one. Rather, a certain ambivalence toward adherents of other faith communities is displayed throughout the Qur'anic text.

It comes therefore as no surprise that such Qur'anic ambiguity is equally mirrored among the global Muslim community. A case in point is the 56 percent of the American Muslim population who—as the same survey brings to light—is more likely than the global median (18 percent) to say that many religions can lead to eternal salvation.[2] In a world of ever-increasing interconnectedness, and a growing presence of Muslims in the Western hemisphere where Muslims work, befriend, and marry non-Muslims, the tendency to advocate such pluralism seems to be emerging. This trend is best reflected now through the rise of contemporary Islamic theologies of religions developed mainly by Muslim scholars living in the Western context.[3] Although premodern Muslim theologians differed on certain subjects, they were united in their rejection of religious pluralism based on Qur'anic evidence and the Prophet's exemplary life (Arabic: *sunna*). Contemporary thinkers such as Seyyed Hossein Nasr, Farid Esack, Abdulaziz Sachedina, or Reza Shah-Kazemi, however, now advocate alternative readings of the Qur'an which part ways from the dominant view that Islam is the final and one true religion.[4]

One major and valid criticism these Muslims must confront is the fact that they tend to sideline Prophet Muhammad's tradition—the second authoritative source in Islam after the Qur'an. The *sunna's* importance cannot be underestimated since it offers Muslims guidance on how certain verses need to be understood. That the *sunna* itself is subject to interpretation does not take away from the fact that Prophet Muhammad did not cease inviting others to embrace Islam while at the same time living amicably with those who did not accept the new faith. The well-known "Constitution of Madina," through which non-Muslims were able to live alongside Muslims, and which until today remains influential in the Muslim discourse on minority rights, is a case in point.[5] Critics argue that Islamic formulations of religious pluralism often do not follow a sound Islamic methodology, giving equal consideration to all major sources of the Islamic tradition: Qur'an, *sunna*, *ijmā'* (consensus of the community or scholars), and *qiyās* (analogical reasoning).[6] Be that as it may, as the central element and primary authority of the Muslim faith, the Qur'an continues to be a key reference for reflecting on interfaith engagement. Notwithstanding the dominant traditional view and mainstream Muslims' claim on Islam being the final religion, the Qur'an is still rich enough to provide plenty of theological resources for engagement with people of other faiths. It is important to preserve the integrity of a tradition with all its truth claims, while at the same time showing that a commitment to interfaith engagement is encouraged *out of that faithfulness* to one's own religion. One notable example of that approach is the Muslim theologian Bediuzzaman Said Nursi (1876–1960), who did not compromise on absolute truth claims. He remained committed to creating faith alliances between Christians and Muslims.[7]

As Yasir Qadhi has pointed out, when Muslim theologians maintain the sovereignty of their own tradition, they are not claiming that *they* are going to heaven and those following other paths are all damned. Rather, what they are asserting is that the *path* they follow leads to God's mercy and that they have no guarantee even about their own fate. This is why, traditionally, Muslims have suspended individual final judgment on these matters, for only God knows the inner state of a human heart and the ultimate destiny of every being, even though a person might look and act non-Islamic from the outside. As Qadhi goes on to say, "This theological claim, however, does not preclude the possibility that well-meaning Others who have never discovered the Islamic path might be saved."[8]

In turning to the Qur'anic text, I aim to identify some of those verses rejecting a passive, arrogant, or isolationist attitude toward others. Needless to say, this exercise is a selective and hence not exhaustive one, given the limitations of this essay. Furthermore, I will not be discussing those critical verses which have challenged interreligious relationships, but will simply offer a personal Muslim rationale for engaging with people of other faiths.

QUR'ANIC REFERENCES FOR INTERFAITH ENGAGEMENT

Some of the essential features of the Qur'an reveal already the unshaken ethical imperative to engage with the whole of humankind. First and foremost, the Qur'an claims to be a message directed to all humanity. In fact, it addresses itself to all creation including the visible realm of this world and the unseen dimension of angels and *jinn*.[9] Transcending ethnic, racial, national, and religious boundaries, the scriptural discourse maintains that all beings are addressed by this eternal divine speech. Qur'an 21:107 puts it quite distinctly: "It was only as a mercy that We[10] sent you [Prophet] to all the worlds."[11] In fact, tribal, linguistic, or religious differences are willed by God, and the Qur'an reminds all humanity to acknowledge this God-given diversity by actively getting to know one another as Qur'an 49:13 declares: "People, We created you all from a single man and a single woman, and made you into races and tribes so that you should get to know one another. In God's eyes, the most honoured of you are the ones most mindful of him: God is all knowing, all aware." Another verse celebrates the linguistic and ethnic diversity of humankind: "Another of his signs is the creation of the heavens and earth, and the diversity of your languages and colours. There truly are signs in this for those who reflect" (Qur'an 30:22). Yet one major Qur'anic passage—Qur'an 5:48—frequently cited in the Muslim discourse on religious pluralism maintains that religious differences were intended by God's wisdom and to test humanity:

> We sent to you [Muhammad] the Scripture with the truth, confirming the Scriptures that came before it, and with final authority over them: so judge between them according to what God has sent down. Do not follow their whims, which deviate from the truth that has come to you. We have assigned a law and a path to each of you. If God had so willed, He would have made you one community, but He wanted to test you through that which He has given you, so race to do good: you will all return to God and He will make clear to you the matters you differed about.

As is evident, the Qur'an is fully aware of these differences and desires communities to compete in goodness and to work for the betterment of humanity. It rejects the notion that these differences define an inherently hostile relationship between Muslims and non-Muslims. This would be a one-sided idea contradicting the many positive examples of interfaith relations throughout history.

The universality of the Qur'an is confirmed even more in the passages dealing with the creation narrative. Qur'an 17:70 states in this respect: "We have honoured the children of Adam and carried them by land and sea; We have provided good sustenance for them and favoured them specially above many of those We have created." First, God himself declares that each and every human being has been honored or, in other words, dignified and raised above all creation. Therefore, the sacredness of every human being, the fundamental dignity of every person, needs to be preserved. To honor such divine sacredness is to engage with every individual on the basis of respect and high opinion. To assume the best in others and to be engaged with them are key attitudes of a Muslim believer. This sanctity also comes through in other Qur'anic creation passages. A rejectionist, intolerant, or exclusionary attitude toward people of other faiths simply neglects such Qur'anic decrees. The verses declare that the human family is one and goes back to one Adamic origin. To be faithful to the Qur'an entails not falling into forgetfulness of these fundamental aspects of human origin, and it entails repeatedly considering the common holy bonds and ties between human beings.

With respect to that, Joseph E. B. Lumbard formulated his ideas on "covenantal pluralism." In Qur'an 7:172 we read: "When your Lord took out the offspring from the loins of the Children of Adam and made them bear witness about themselves, He said, 'Am I not your Lord?' and they replied, 'Yes, we bear witness.' So you cannot say on the Day of Resurrection, 'We were not aware of this.'" This declaration of "yes," according to Lumbard, is just a reaffirmation of an initial, primordial covenant. This covenant, which took place between God and his people, was made before humans were here in this world and is expanded to all humanity. All humans bear the imprint of the initial pre-temporal covenant within, so all are held accountable.[12] Knowing that all human beings carry this sacred imprint simply confirms the worth and value of all people and hence should be taken as a major stimulus to be open for interfaith engagement.

Such a God-given worth and value is reiterated through passages narrating that God has breathed into humans something from his own spirit (Arabic: *rūḥ*). Qur'an 38:71–85 tells the creation story as follows:

> Your Lord said to the angels, "I will create a human being from clay. When I have shaped him and breathed from My Spirit (*rūḥī*) into him, bow down before him." The angels all bowed down together, but not Iblīs [Satan], who was too proud. He became a rebel. God said, "Iblīs, what prevents you from bowing down to the human being I have made with My own hands? Are you too high and mighty?" Iblīs said, "I am better than him: You made me from fire, and him from clay." "Get out of here! You are rejected: My rejection will follow you till the Day of Judgment!" but Iblīs said, "My Lord, grant me respite until the Day when they are raised from the dead," so He said, "You have respite till the Appointed Day." Iblīs said, "I swear by your might! I will tempt all but Your chosen servants." God said, "This is the truth—I speak only the truth—I will fill Hell with you and all those that follow you."

In a very intimate and personal way, God creates Adam with his own two hands. Adam in the Islamic tradition is considered to be the progenitor of all humankind, and thus all descriptions in this creation account apply to everyone as well. Moreover, the human being is honored by being endowed with the divine spirit—sacredness infuses his whole being. The reaction of Iblīs is anything but honorable. He refuses to surrender to God's will and decision and asserts an arrogant attitude. Here it is noteworthy that Iblīs, as Muslim tradition explains, was a pious *jinn* who because of his extraordinary devotion to God was elevated to the ranks of the angels. Muslim theologians have reflected on this attitude of religious arrogance. Iblīs is a believer but still falls prey to an exclusionary and haughty behavior based on his own logic. At the end, God rejects him. Taking the Qur'anic story to heart, Muslims are reminded that it can be easy to fall victim to such an Iblīsi logic by claiming superiority over others who do not follow one's personal preferences. The Qur'an simply states that the way to honor God is to honor his creation. Engaging with people of other faiths is one way to demonstrate such love and loyalty for God. Some examples in today's media show how those Muslims who follow in the footsteps of Iblīs can behave. They have no regard for the sacredness of human beings and sadly continue killing innocent people. Behind such crimes lies the wrong and arrogant conviction that one is better and more valuable than others who do not deserve to live. As Iblīs states in his response, he will only tempt those who lack sincerity and genuine love for God.

Furthermore, the Qur'an is deeply dialogical in its approach towards its listeners. The revelation is responsive to people from various backgrounds: Jews, Christians, polytheists—all find themselves being addressed by the Qur'anic discourse. The persistent form "They say x; Say to them y" mirrors this interactive dimension of the revelation. Even on occasions when the Qur'an's credibility is questioned, rejected, or met with denial and ridicule, its engagement with humanity does not cease. Taken together, the Qur'an as a "book of guidance" (Arabic: *kitāb al-hudā*), and the Prophet Muhammad as God's messenger, maintain an active, dynamic, and non-isolationist attitude toward a varied audience. Muslims who claim to believe in the Qur'an and who have internalized its message cannot but embody its overall open approach toward others.

This is not to say that the Qur'an embraces every idea or

behavior. To the contrary, Scripture continuously challenges, criticizes, or refutes certain positions while remaining attentive and open to dialogue. In this sense, the Qur'an displays a very realistic outlook. Those who claim to hold the truth and other solutions in balance will likewise be comfortable with an uncomfortable dialectic. The Qur'an models such behavior to its followers so that they do not shy away from difficult debates. Hence, the reader encounters in the text many passages which invite healthy questioning, reflection, and argumentation. For example, Qur'an 16:125 exhorts Muhammad and all Muslims in the following: "[Prophet] call people to the way of your Lord with wisdom and good teaching. Argue with them in the most courteous way, for your Lord knows best who has strayed from his way and who is rightly guided." Even in the case of Pharaoh, who claimed divinity, the Qur'an recalls how to respond properly: "Go, both of you [Moses and Aaron], to Pharaoh for he has exceeded all bounds. Speak to him gently so that he may take heed, or show respect" (Qur'an 20:43–44). To be wise, cordial, gentle, and humble when entering a dialogue of faith with another person are Qur'anic virtues, and they go against all attitudes of religious arrogance and harsh behavior. Instead, the truth should humble people by alerting them to be fully aware of the great burden and responsibility toward others.

Further, multiple instances in the Qur'an offer guidance that interfaith engagement is intrinsic and critical to the Qur'an's self-understanding. Time and again, the Qur'an reminds its readers to remember the prophetic figures of the past who received revelation from God. The Qur'anic discourse declares itself to be the final message of a primordial faith revealed throughout human history to a number of prophets. As Qur'an 42:13 says: "In matters of faith, he has laid down for you [people] the same commandment that he gave Noah, which We have revealed to you [Muhammad] and which We enjoined on

Abraham and Moses and Jesus: 'Uphold the faith and do not divide into factions within it.' " Adam, Abraham, Noah, Moses, and Jesus are among the twenty-eight messengers mentioned by name in Scripture. The Qur'an assumes that its audience already has a familiarity with these biblical figures as it does not offer details on their lives but simply uses the recurring formula, "And remember [Noah, Lot, Moses] etc." Some examples can be found repeatedly in chapter 21. For instance Qur'an 21:48 states: "We gave Moses and Aaron [the Scripture] that distinguishes right from wrong, a light and a reminder for those who are mindful of God." Or Qur'an 21:78: "And remember David and Solomon, when they gave judgment regarding the field into which some people's sheep strayed by night and grazed. We witnessed their judgment." Similarly, Qur'an 21:89–90 reads: "Remember Zachariah, when he cried to his Lord, 'My Lord, do not leave me childless, though You are the best of heirs.' We answered him—We gave him John, curing his wife [for him]—they were always keen to do good deeds. They called upon Us out of longing and awe, and humbled themselves before Us."

As such, the reader is expected to engage with the lives of previous messengers and the revelations they received from God and to reflect on the moral teachings of these Prophetic narratives. In fact, one of the fundamental articles of faith derived from the Qur'an is the full belief in all of the messengers of God, beginning from Adam up until Muhammad, as Qur'an 2:285–286 puts it: "The Messenger believes in what has been sent down to him from his Lord, as do the faithful. They all believe in God, his angels, his scriptures, and his messengers. 'We make no distinction between any of his messengers,' they say. 'We hear and obey. Grant us Your forgiveness, our Lord. To You we all return!' "

Belief in these messengers means also being approachable and welcoming to their followers and showing a willingness to create an atmosphere of trust and respect in which learning, listening, and inquiry are possible. The Qur'an instructs Muslims to dialogue with Jews and Christians—the "People of the Book" as the Qur'an calls them—in the fairest manner. It sets forth both the etiquette and theology of dialogue: "[Believers] argue only in the best way with the People of the Book, except with those of them who act unjustly. Say, 'We believe in what was revealed to us and in what was revealed to you; our God and your God is one [and the same]; we are devoted to him'" (Qur'an 29:46).

Despite the fact that the Qur'an frequently charges that other faith communities have distorted or altered previous messages, it continues to confirm their validity and truth from God. The Qur'an claims to have been revealed as a book confirming all previous scriptures, but particularly the Torah, the Psalms, and the gospel. With respect to that, Qur'an 3:3–4 asserts: "Step by step, he has sent the Scripture down to you [Prophet] with the Truth, confirming what went before: he sent down the Torah and the Gospel earlier as a guide for people and he has sent down the distinction [between right and wrong]. Those who deny God's revelations will suffer severe torment: God is almighty and capable of retribution."

Hence, Muslims who aim to take these verses seriously should remain open for dialogue with different faith communities and should not close doors because some ideas might feel discomforting. This is an attitude of mercy and compassion— two key names of God which are mentioned at the beginning of every chapter of the Qur'an except chapter nine, in the widely used formula of the *basmala*, "In the Name of God, The Lord of Mercy, The Giver of Mercy." Mercy entails that each and every individual creates a warm and inviting personal space and behavior so that others feel comfortable approaching and consulting a Muslim on any matter. Here again, one finds the Qur'an to be advocating this spirit: "Out of mercy from God, you Prophet were gentle in your dealings with them—had you been harsh, or hard-hearted, they would have dispersed and left you—so pardon them and ask forgiveness for them. Consult with them about matters, then, when you have decided on a course of action, put your trust in God: God loves those who put their trust in him" (Qur'an 3:159).

The Qur'an not only recognizes religious diversity and hands down the norms that should administer interreligious relations; it also calls for respect and protection of all places of worship. Qur'an 22:40 maintains: "Those who have been driven unjustly from their homes only for saying, 'Our Lord is God.' If God did not repel some people by means of others, many monasteries, churches, synagogues, and mosques, where God's name is much invoked, would have been destroyed. God is sure to help those who help his cause—God is strong and mighty." If the destruction, desecration, or vandalism of religious houses of worship represents a gross violation of Islamic principles, how can Islam ever endorse the neglect or disregard of humans equipped with the divine spark? A Muslim should therefore strive to build bridges of understanding and mutual respect instead of holding or fostering views degrading others. The Prophet himself followed this Qur'anic rule by giving permission to a delegation of the Christians of Najrān to pray in his mosque in Medina. He went even further by calling them and the Muslims to this Qur'anic decree: "Say, 'People of the Book, let us arrive at a statement that is common to us all: we worship God alone, we ascribe no partner to him, and none of us takes others beside God as lords.' If they turn away, say 'Witness our devotion to him'" (Qur'an 3:64). It is quite telling that one of the major dialogue initiatives, A Common Word, started by Muslims has taken this Qur'anic proclamation as its foundational principle.[13]

Christians, as the Qur'an tells its audience, are considered to be the nearest in amity to Muslims. It is because of their piety and humility that they are regarded as special:

> You are sure to find that the closest in affection towards the believers are those who say, "We are Christians," for there are among them people devoted to learning and ascetics. These people are not given to arrogance, and when they listen to what has been sent down to the Messenger, you will see their eyes overflowing with tears because they recognize the Truth [in it]. They say, "Our Lord, we believe, so count us amongst the witnesses." (Qur'an 5:82–83)

This special relationship with Christians does not mean that Muslims have not engaged with other faith communities. To the contrary, the legal term of *ahl al-kitāb* (People of the Book) has come to embrace other communities as well after Muslims entered new territories and encountered other religious traditions. For centuries, therefore, Muslims were able to live alongside Hindus, Buddhists, and the followers of other religions in the Asian context.

CONCLUSION

The Qur'an provides a rich theological repertoire for articulating specific principles for promoting interfaith engagement. Interreligious conversation is intrinsic to the nature of the Qur'an and should ideally be a basic feature in every Muslim's life. As noted earlier, the Qur'an models such initiatives throughout its discourse. Early Muslim scholarship showed enthusiasm and curiosity to engage with extra-Qur'anic sources such as the Hebrew or the Christian Bible. For these Muslims, sacred knowledge bringing one closer to the divine should be taken wherever it may be found. This has not meant, though, giving up on one's principles of faith or compromising on certain beliefs. Instead, it was a natural attitude emanating from the Qur'an which established a kinship with previous revelations. That the Near Eastern context, as the common origin of Judaism, Christianity, and Islam, represents this only too well is often dismissed. Sadly, today such intellectual exercises are rare to find. To cite the survey mentioned at the beginning of this chapter, in only three of the thirty-seven countries where the question was asked do at least half of Muslims say they know a great deal or something about Christian beliefs and practices.[14] Such religious illiteracy can be dangerous and prone to create tensions and hostilities in the long run.

Many may be trying to reconcile the apparent disconnect between these Qur'anic principles enunciated above with disturbing contemporary practices of violence carried out in the name of Islam. Concluding thoughts by Qur'an scholar Ingrid Mattson can shed light on this predicament and offer a balanced and hopeful prospect on the future:

> From the time Mu'awiya's troops raised pages of the Qur'an on their lances to the start of the first Gulf War in 1991, when Saddam Hussein put the Qur'anic phrase *Allahu akbar,* "God is greater," on the Iraqi flag, up to the international terrorist movements of our time, there have been Muslims who have used the Qur'an to encourage, justify, and challenge political agendas, some violent and intolerant. At the same time, there have been more Muslims who have been inspired by the Qur'an to pay charity, be generous, establish peace treaties, and work for a just and accountable political order.

In Muslim societies in which religious identity is strong, the language of the Qur'an is the dominant and normative discourse, and some will use the Qur'an in a manipulative fashion, while others will sincerely try to be guided by its message. It is impossible to prevent the Qur'an from being "used" to justify bad behavior. Shakespeare said that "the devil can cite scripture for his purpose," and this is as true for the Qur'an as it is of the Bible, which has been used at various times to justify everything from the enslavement of Africans to the subjugation of women and the forcible expulsion of indigenous peoples from their lands.[15]

QUESTIONS FOR DISCUSSION

1. What are some of the scriptural resources in your own tradition encouraging interfaith conversation?

2. How do we approach scriptural passages in our traditions that do not promote dialogue?

3. Do you believe that such scriptural tension between texts that encourage interfaith conversation and texts that discourage it can be solved?

NOTES

1. For more details see *The World's Muslims: Religion, Politics, and Society*, April 30, 2013 (Washington, DC: The Pew Forum on Religion and Public Life, 2013), http://www.pewforum.org/files/2013/04/worlds-muslims-religion-politics-society-full-report.pdf.

2. Ibid., 140.

3. See for instance Mun'im Sirry, *Scriptural Polemics: The Qur'ān and Other Religions* (Oxford: Oxford University Press, 2014); Jerusha Tanner Lamptey, *Never Wholly Other: A Muslima Theology of Religious Pluralism* (Oxford: Oxford University Press, 2014); Mohammad

Hassan Khalil, *Islam and the Fate of Others: The Salvation Question* (Oxford: Oxford University Press, 2012).

4. For a broad spectrum of perspectives on the subject of Islam and salvation, see *Between Heaven and Hell: Islam, Salvation, and the Fate of Others*, ed. Mohammad Hassan Khalil (Oxford: Oxford University Press, 2013).

5. For the detailed content of this document, see Michael Lecker, *The Constitution of Medina: Muḥammad's First Legal Document* (Princeton, NJ: Darwin Press, 2004).

6. See for example the criticism that such scholarly activity does not respect the well-defined parameters of the traditional Islamic sciences: Andrew Booso, "The Finality of Islam—With Reference to Perennial Philosophy," October 18, 2011, http://www.virtualmosque.com/islam-studies/islamic-law/the-finality-of-islam-with-reference-to-perennial-philosophy/.

7. For more on his thoughts and practices, especially regarding Christian-Muslim collaboration, see the standard intellectual biography by Şükran Vahide, *Islam in Modern Turkey: An Intellectual Biography of Bediuzzaman Said Nursi* (Albany: State University of New York Press, 2005).

8. Yasir Qadhi, "The Path of Allah or the Paths of Allah? Revisiting Classical and Medieval Sunni Approaches to the Salvation of Others," in Khalil, *Between Heaven and Hell*, 119–21.

9. The term *jinn* refers to a community of supernatural beings who, similar to humans, can distinguish between right and wrong and who are specifically mentioned in Scripture as those who receive revelation as guidance. The well-known word "genius" is derived from the *jinn*.

10. The *We* in the Qur'an is the so-called magisterial or royal *We* referring to God. In the Qur'an it is quite usual that the divine voice switches between the uses of the first-person singular ("I") and the first-person plural ("We") when referring to God.

11. In the following, I use the Qur'an translation by M. A. S.

Abdel Haleem, *The Qur'an: English Translation and Parallel Arabic Text* (Oxford: Oxford University Press, 2010).

12. For more details, see Joseph E. B. Lumbard, "Covenant and Covenants in the Qur'an," www.academia.edu/8807609/Covenant_and_Covenants_in_the_Quran.

13. For more on "A Common Word" initiative, see www.acommonword.com.

14. *The World's Muslims*, 118.

15. Ingrid Mattson, *The Story of the Qur'an: Its History and Place in Muslim Life*, 2d ed. (Malden, MA: Wiley-Blackwell, 2013), 193.

Part Two

VOICES OF
FAITHFUL NEIGHBORS

3

SURVEYING A CHURCH'S ATTITUDE TOWARD AND INTERACTION WITH ISLAM

~

David Gortner

Virginia Theological Seminary invited our alumni, as well as other lay and ordained church leaders affiliated with the seminary, to participate in an online survey about their interfaith experience.[1] We asked them in particular about the following, in relation to Islam specifically as well as other faiths in general:

- *Interfaith formation and education*: Whether or not, and how, they learned about other faiths
- *Interfaith instruction and engagement in congregations*: Their experiences teaching about other faiths in, and inviting other faith leaders into, their congregations
- *Interfaith partnership in the broader community*: Their experiences engaging in interfaith work and partnerships in their neighborhoods, towns, and cities
- *Evangelism*: Their experiences fostering direct efforts

in their congregations to speak more publicly about their faith and experience of God

- *Theological differences and similarities*: Their views of similarities and differences between Muslim and Christian theology
- *Goals and plans*: Their hopes, aims, and plans regarding evangelism, interfaith education, and interfaith relations
- *Demographics*: Their age and gender, size and location of their congregation, and distance to the nearest mosque and another faith's house of worship

From an initial email invitation, we secured 353 survey responses (nearly a 9 percent response rate from the total pool of recipients, but closer to a 15 percent response rate among alumni). The degree of survey completion varied: more than three hundred completed the first twelve survey questions, more than two hundred wrote thoughtful responses to later open-ended questions, and 265 completed the basic demographic information at the end of the survey.

Survey respondents were from all regions of the United States and from other countries in a pattern of distribution reflecting the geographic spread of the seminary's alumni—most in the southern and northeast United States and only a few (eight people) in other countries. Most were ordained, with 15 percent identifying themselves as lay leaders. Nearly two-thirds of respondents were men. Similar to the racial distribution of clergy and laity in The Episcopal Church, 92 percent were white. Only 14 percent were under the age of 35; an additional 21 percent were between 35 and 49; and 40 percent were 50 to 64. One-fourth were 65 or older. Nearly three-fourths were serving in urban or suburban settings; the remaining respondents were in small towns or rural areas. These distributions of race, age, gender, and setting of ministry among the seminary's survey respondents are consistent with the patterns found over-all in The Episcopal Church across the United States—and are consistent with patterns found among several of the mainline Protestant denominations in the United States.[2]

The following discussion of survey results is restricted to the 222 alumni priests whose responses were most complete across all segments of the survey. These respondents represent not only active clergy graduates of Virginia Theological Seminary but those who had served or were currently serving in congregations, schools, and other ministry settings throughout The Episcopal Church.

Two Key Findings

Let us begin with a few vivid patterns emerging from survey responses. Two key findings emerged:

1. A solid majority of the seminary's active alumni priests have pursued some education in Islam and other religions.
2. This exposure does not consistently lead to action in the form of parish programs for interreligious education or cooperative interfaith engagement.

Nearly three-quarters of active clergy respondents indicated having some education in Islam, and just over three-quarters indicated education in other religions. But only around half of these priests have held forums or instructional events in their parishes about Islam or other religions. Furthermore, the total of priests who have successfully partnered with leaders or congregations of other faiths on various interfaith activities in their surrounding communities was only 38 percent (see table 1).[3]

There are a few things to note about this pattern. First, for

	Did you **have some education** about . . . ? (% yes)	Have you **led forums or instruction** about . . . ? (% yes)	Have you **partnered with** leaders or congregations of **other faiths** on various activities? (% yes)
Islam	71%	50%	
			38%
Other faiths	76%	47%	

Table 1: Responses to three key questions about interfaith learning, teaching, and partnership (165 active priests)

the seminary and for The Episcopal Church as a whole, these results are encouraging: more than three-quarters of currently active priests have had at least some education about and exposure to Islam. Around half have taught in their congregations at some point about Islam. And while only a little more than one-third of clergy have successfully involved their congregations in partnerships with congregations of other faiths, this is still much higher than the average interfaith involvement of U.S. Christian congregations found in the *Faith Communities Today* survey of 2010.[4] Furthermore, this pattern in Episcopal priests' responses held constant across clergy gender, race, age, and geographic location in the United States. It appears that The Episcopal Church is doing well compared with other denominations when it comes to fostering interfaith understanding and cooperation.

It is worth noting the gaps. There is a marked disparity between priests' education about Islam and other faiths, their efforts in teaching in their congregations about Islam and other faiths, and their successful efforts in forming any partnerships or collaborative actions with congregations of faiths outside the Christian tradition. What contributes to the gap between church leaders' interreligious education and their efforts to provide opportunities for education and engagement in their parishes?

Before we explore this question more fully, I can point to three main factors that influence an Episcopal congregation's degree of involvement in interreligious education and partnerships: the prior education of the church's leaders (particularly its priests), those leaders' theological beliefs about points of similarity and difference between Christianity and other faiths, and the Episcopal congregation's geographic proximity to a non-Christian congregation. There is also a direct relationship between church leaders' instruction and training of congregations in evangelism and their instruction about Muslims and people of other faiths: stronger evangelism and stronger interfaith education seem to go hand in hand.

Finally, these yes-no survey questions were broadly worded, allowing for any level of learning, teaching, and partnership to be endorsed positively, no matter how meager or momentous the effort. Thus, the positive responses may actually mask a percentage of "better than nothing" responses by priests whose efforts have been minimal but who have at least done something. I will address this point specifically in the next section, through a closer examination of survey responses.

CHRISTIAN CLERGY'S INTERRELIGIOUS PERSONAL LEARNING, CONGREGATIONAL INSTRUCTION, AND CROSS-CONGREGATION PARTNERSHIPS

Levels of Clergy Learning about Islam and other Faiths

We asked two questions about Islam specifically and again more generally about other faiths, one pointing toward intentional seeking of instruction in a more structured group setting through courses or lectures, and another pointing toward intentional self-directed learning through direct reading and study of another religion's sacred texts. With regard to intentional instruction, fewer than three-quarters of active priests (71 percent) reported some form of course- or lecture-based education in Islam. With regard to self-directed learning, 76 percent reported having read at least some portion of the Qur'an. Regarding other faiths (primarily Judaism, Hinduism, and Buddhism), 76 percent reported that they had taken courses or lectures, and 69 percent indicated having read sacred texts of other faith traditions.

At first glance, this looks rather positive: around 70 percent of Episcopal priests, themselves called and pledged to committed study and teaching of Christian Scripture, have sought some level of knowledge about Islam and other religions. However, only 25 percent of the seminary's alumni priests indicated that they have read "significant portions" of the Qur'an, while 51 percent reported they have read "a few verses"—a far more cursory exposure. Additionally, priests' open-ended explanations about the other religious texts they have read ranged from minimal to moderate engagement: "I have heard them read publicly at interfaith services," "Bhagavad Gita—portions of it," and "Hebrew Bible, and selected midrashim" indicate a more minimal level of exposure; "the Bhagavad Gita, some Baha'i scripture, some from the Book of Mormon" indicates a little bit deeper and broader engagement; but "the Upanishads, the Bhagavad Gita, the Tao Te Ching, devotional and mystical poetry from various traditions" shows exposure beyond a cursory level. This indicates at best a passing knowledge of the scriptures or core texts of other religions. As stated by one priest, "I answered yes, but the portion of other sacred texts I have been exposed to is very insignificant."

Beyond direct reading of sacred texts, education varied widely in breadth and depth, from formal courses to single lectures, public-broadcasting programs, self-directed reading, travel or residence in foreign countries, visits at worship services, formal interfaith dialogues, and informal conversations with non-Christian believers. A high percentage of the seminary's active ordained alumni reported having taken a world religions course in seminary or in college, and others reported specific courses in Eastern religions, Islam, or Judaism.

Personal contact with other believers or living in a country with a different majority religion had a particularly strong impact. This was especially true in regard to Islam, as indicated by these two priests:

> Working with Islamic teachers and community leaders has been the most helpful for me. I can research and teach the tenets of other faiths, but to work with others who actually live out a life based in a different faith was very helpful to me emotionally and spiritually.

> Living with Muslims in a country with Muslim leadership [was especially helpful]—by talking with Muslims . . . hearing their perspectives, and reading the Qur'an and commentaries that explain the historical background, I can better understand what the Prophet said and meant.

This final quote shows a level of profoundly deep engagement, in which a priest took the opportunity of immersion in a Muslim context not only to engage vigorously in dialogue but also to immerse himself in the Qur'an, hadith, and other commentaries. For this priest, the level of interfaith understanding has reached a deep level, rare among clergy.

Despite the wide range of exposure, most alumni of this seminary appear to have gained some level of interreligious exposure through courses, texts, and other sources of learning. How then does such preparation influence ministry in Episcopal parishes?

Level of Instruction about Islam and Other
Faiths Offered by Clergy in Congregations

Although two-thirds to three-quarters of Episcopal Church leaders (at least from this seminary) have sought or received education in other religions, only half have taught or held forums about Islam (50 percent) or other religions (47 percent) in their congregations.

A closer examination reveals once again a range in depth and breadth of teaching. Of the priests who taught about religions other than Islam, more than half (60 percent) focused on Judaism, while only about a quarter (27 percent) focused on Buddhism and less than a fifth (17 percent) focused on Hinduism. About 15 percent offered instruction in all of these faiths and more in an introduction to "world religions." Interreligious classes at times were for adults, at other times for youth, or, at a regional level, for people learning to do ministry. Motivations for offering interreligious instruction in Episcopal congregations included personal and congregational interest, the need to address public events and issues (such as September 11), concern for neighbors in faith and for healthy civic relationships, and enrichment of understanding of the Christian faith by way of comparison. A few seminary alumni noted that their educational efforts about other faiths were motivated by a desire to help their congregants become better apologists and witnesses: "The primary purpose of such educational programs was to assist our people in understanding what other faiths believe as compared to the Christian faith," wrote one respondent.

"The secondary purpose was to assist our people in witnessing to adherents of those faiths in a winsome manner." There is some risk in interreligious instruction motivated solely by a desire for proclamation (perhaps bordering on proselytizing) without an equally strong desire for dialogue.

The priests who did not offer interreligious instruction gave a range of reasons for not providing such instruction. Their reasons included a more significant concern about lack of congregants' knowledge about their own Christian faith, other priorities in ministry taking primary focus, lack of personal or congregational interest, and lack of time. These reasons may have some legitimacy at times and in some places, but at other times they may also simply be excuses. Lack of time, resources, knowledge, and interest can also be recited as reasons for inattention to prayer, evangelism and outreach, self-care, or many other important elements of Christian life that require ministerial and instructional effort.

However, these priests raise an important concern that their congregants understand their own Christian faith more deeply. This concern coincides with an enduring challenge in The Episcopal Church and many Christian denominations of low attendance at adult educational forums and sessions. If people will not commit time and invest effort in deeper learning about their own faith, then interreligious education sinks even lower on the priority list. These priests are fighting an uphill battle for their congregants' interest.

Unfortunately, such a situation can press a desperate religious leader toward either-or assumptions about how people learn. "How can I teach about Islam or some other religion when people don't understand so many things about their own Christian faith?" a leader might ask. This desperate plea signals a blinding of pedagogical imagination. People do not simply learn in a tightly compartmentalized subject-by-subject manner. What we learn in one arena helps enrich our learning in other arenas. Lessons about governments in other nations through history help American high school students better understand what they have heard and studied in American government classes. Learning another language enriches knowledge and appreciation of one's native tongue, as one discovers differences in nuances of meaning. The same overlap occurs with interreligious education, especially when done with planned attention to the overlaps. An introduction to Islam for Christians not only increases understanding of Muslims, it deepens Christian self-understanding. Even more, encounters with people of other faiths and hearing their perceptions of Christianity can help Christians learn to listen more generously to others and to think more clearly about their own faith. One priest described her discovery about the surprising value of interreligious instruction in a setting where such interest was not expected:

> I was surprised how well an interspiritual book study (at my previous small town, southern parish) on *God of Love: A Journey to the Heart of Judaism, Christianity, and Islam* by Mirabai Starr was received. People love discovering our commonalities (and differences), and the deep points of connection in our social justice and mystical streams of teaching. I found that people were more ready than I imagined for an interspiritual understanding of our traditions rooted in a vision of our shared, global humanity.

In contrast to withdrawal from interreligious instruction are the examples of priests who with their congregations have gone the extra mile to create rich learning opportunities for their congregations and other people from the surrounding community about other religions. The most robust forms of interreligious education involve more than classroom presentations and discussions—they involve direct exposure to and interaction with other communities of faith. The following quotes offer two particularly strong examples of how this more thorough and intensive interreligious instruction can be offered for congregations:

> We held a forum on how a Christian might approach learning from other faiths. We are also involved in a project led by a sister parish fifteen minutes away that is hosting dialogue encounters with a regional Islamic center.

> We do an interfaith tour every year with the confirmation class—a Christian place of worship (varies from year to year, last year was Moravian), the Islamic house of prayer, and Temple Emmanuel. We take three weeks beforehand talking about what we share and where we differ and all have the opportunity to explore and ask questions.

These two examples help highlight the tremendous value that comes to Christians from interacting with Muslims and with people from other religious traditions. Classroom presentation and discussion are combined effectively in these examples with opportunities for cross-faith conversation and planned visits to worship and educational gatherings of other religious communities. It is through this direct experience of, exposure to, and interaction with people of other faiths that the material presented and discussed in classes or forums becomes more deeply anchored.

One way to provide this opportunity for cross-faith exposure and interaction is through lectures, classes, or sermons in Christian congregations by clergy or lay leaders from other faith traditions. More than half (54 percent) of the seminary's alumni priests affirmed that they bring clergy or lay leaders from other faiths to speak to their congregations. As priests indicated in their comments, such visiting speakers are openly welcomed and eagerly engaged by people in Episcopal congregations.

> We've invited many scholars from Islamic and Jewish traditions to come and speak. They tend to be well received.

> Warmly received the Muslim representatives. Warmly celebrated having a rabbi teach a bit of Old Testament to our adults.

There are particularly creative examples of effective involvement of visiting speakers in the educational efforts of a congregation. The following example shows how a priest made effective use of connections in the broader community to identify a married couple from different religious traditions who could talk about religious faithfulness in the multifaith contexts of household and public life.

> We first did this in response to September 11 (in a previous parish, much larger than my current one, in suburban Virginia) when I had to boycott the community prayer service because other leaders refused to invite the imam. My parish fully supported me but had a lot of questions, so I invited our local director of public health, and a doctor who happened to be a Muslim and married to a

> Christian, both from the Middle East. They worked
> with me to lead a very good series on the basics of
> Islam, and how a Muslim/Christian relationship
> works in a home and could work in a community.
> In my current parish I have also had a series on the
> life of the Prophet, and one on the basics shared by
> the three Abrahamic faiths.

This priest and lay leaders of this congregation took seriously the affront of exclusion in a broader community's moments of public prayer and sought to address the issue through vigorous education of the congregation. The priest has carried that concern with him through his continuing ministry in other congregations.

Of course, there is always the risk of offense that can come with the invitation of a speaker from another faith tradition—either offense of one's congregation, or offense of the visiting speaker. The following quote offers an example of how an otherwise positive encounter can go sour.

> Twenty-plus years ago I had a professor from Mary
> Washington University come and speak on Islam.
> He was originally from Iran and had been in the
> United States twenty-five years. It went well until he
> said that the Qur'an gave men permission to strike
> their wives to discipline them, and he went on to
> say that women should not be educated to be doc-
> tors and engineers.

Potential for such offense is not by any means restricted to visiting speakers from other faith traditions. It is quite possible for an ecumenical visitor from another Christian tradition, or a visiting priest or deacon, or a speaker from one's own congregation, or (dare I say it) a bishop to speak words and ideas that offend. The crucial matter is how one prepares a visiting speaker and congregation and how one engages the ideas shared.

Clergy can opt for offering interreligious instruction themselves ("in-house"), or for bringing clergy or leaders from other faith traditions into their congregations as visiting speakers or preachers to offer instruction—or, as indicated in some of the examples above, they can combine both of these approaches. The examples cited suggest that the combined approach may be particularly effective.

Between these two approaches, two-thirds of the seminary's alumni priests find ways of providing interreligious education for their congregations, either teaching about other religions themselves or inviting clergy or leaders from other religions to teach. One-third of those responding to the survey do neither—and, interestingly, most of these also do nothing to develop their congregations' capacities in evangelism. But more than one-third (37 percent) are combining both approaches to interreligious instruction. These priests see no discord between Christian formation and instruction about other religions; indeed, they recognize how a solid introduction and discussion about other religions combined with opportunities for interaction with adherents to other religions can help anchor and solidify Episcopalians' Christian religious identity while also helping build mutual understanding and capacity for addressing common concerns.

Level of Congregational Partnerships and Collaborations with Muslims and Other Faith Communities

Constructive interfaith relations can be fostered through a wide range of connections and events, beginning with invitations between clergy or lay leaders to offer instruction, pulpit exchanges, interfaith prayer services on days of remembrance or other holidays, participation in interfaith alliances for social outreach or action, and specific partnerships between congregations for the sake of public ministry. While 59 percent of the seminary's alumni priests are involved in an interfaith organization, association, or network, and 54 percent have invited other religious leaders to teach or preach, only 38 percent have partnered actively with congregations of other faiths (primarily Jewish or Muslim) in some shared experience of prayer, conversation, fellowship, service and outreach, or advocacy. It certainly requires greater effort to pursue and support interreligious collaborations between congregations—similar to the effort required in bringing together neighboring Christian congregations for shared events and experiences. It is easier and more readily attainable to arrange visits of single leaders from one congregation to another, or to meet as leaders with one another in interfaith organizations, than it is to plan for shared events, partnerships, and sustained activities between congregations. And yet, relationships and mutual understanding cannot easily be strengthened simply by a visit from a leader of another faith tradition, or by leaders engaging only one another in conversation. This is precisely the reason for the resolution adopted at the 2012 General Convention of The Episcopal Church that all members of the church be actively involved in interreligious work.[5]

But such interfaith partnership for Christian congregations goes hand in hand with their interreligious education— and both are influenced significantly by their clergy. Episcopal priests who offered interreligious education about Islam or other faiths in their congregations were twice as likely to get involved with other religious leaders in interfaith associations, networks, or organizations. Conversely, priests *not* offering interreligious education in their congregations were nearly three times *less* likely to engage their congregations in active partnership with other non-Christian faith communities. A sim-

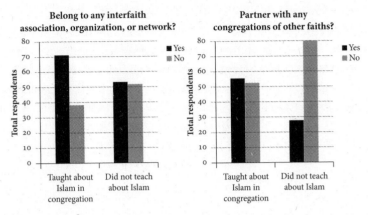

Figures 1 and 2

ilar pattern holds when considering the education and exposure that a visiting ordained or lay leader from another faith can offer. Priests who invited Muslims or other faith leaders to speak at their congregations were more than twice as likely also to join interfaith networks or associations, and those who had never invited other faith leaders to teach or preach at their congregations were three times less likely to help form partnerships between their congregations and other non-Christian faith communities. Putting it simply, teaching a congregation about Islam and other faiths goes hand in hand with belonging to an interfaith association and not teaching a congregation about Islam decreases the already low likelihood of interreligious partnership between congregations.

WHAT INFLUENCES INTERRELIGIOUS EDUCATION AND PARTNERSHIP IN CHRISTIAN CONGREGATIONS?

Geography and Proximity

Mosques and Islamic centers are still relatively rare on the American landscape compared with Jewish synagogues, but their frequency is increasing. Reflecting the increasing diversity of contemporary religious life, more than 60 percent of priest respondents were in parishes located within ten miles of a mosque, and 82 percent were within ten miles of another non-Christian house of worship. Still, as figure 3 shows, there were many priest respondents (about 30 percent) serving congregations where the nearest mosque or Islamic center was more than twenty miles away. By far, the vast majority of American congregations most distant from a mosque or Islamic center are in rural or small-town settings, while those closest to a mosque or Islamic center are mostly in urban or suburban settings. Rural and small-town congregations also tend to be smaller in membership. Outside of urban areas, very few Episcopal congregations have more than 250 member households. The largest Episcopal congregations are in cities and suburbs. As one might expect, this proximity has a direct impact on interreligious instruction and partnership—as the saying goes, "out of sight, out of mind." As one rural priest said, "I serve a small, rural congregation. Other than the Mormon church, the nearest non-Christian faith (Jewish, Buddhist, Islamic, etc.) is

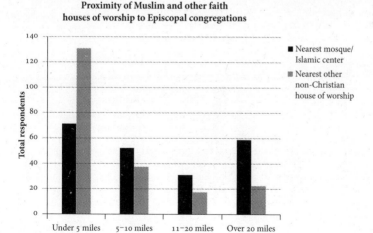

Figure 3

about one hour away. My congregation has evinced no interest in other faiths to this point."

Proximity makes a difference. As might be suspected, Episcopal congregations closer to a mosque or Islamic center (which also tend to be larger) are more likely to offer forums or classes about Islam, to invite other faith leaders to teach or preach, to have opportunities to learn how to share their own faith, and to enter into interreligious partnerships with congregations of other faith traditions. Additionally, their priests are much more likely to get involved in interfaith associations or networks. But, interestingly, the priests in these congregations are no more (or less) likely to have taken classes about or studied the sacred texts of Islam or other faiths.

Proximity increases the likelihood of interreligious relationship. And congregational size is closely related to proximity to non-Christian houses of worship, because larger congregations are much more frequently in urban and suburban locations. So, as might be expected, congregational size does indeed make a difference in interfaith education and relationships. As seen in figure 4, priests serving smaller "family-size" congre-

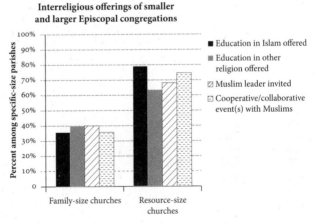

Figure 4

gations (one hundred or fewer households) were least likely to offer instruction about Islam or to engage their congregations in Muslim-Christian cooperative events, while those serving larger "resource-size" congregations (five hundred or more households) were most likely to offer education about Islam and collaboration with Muslims in ministry.

Clergy Interreligious Learning

Priests' prior education in Islam or in other faiths has a direct impact on their offering some educational programs in the parish or other ministry setting. As shown in figure 5, of those who taught or held forums about Islam, 80 percent had previously taken a course or received education in that religion. The remaining 20 percent who taught or held forums about Islam did so without benefit of such previous education, and one may ponder what information was conveyed in these cases. Put simply, education in Islam increases the likelihood that priests will offer their congregations such instruction, while an absence of education about Islam increases the likelihood that priests will not approach the subject of Islam with their congregations.

There was an even clearer relationship between priests'

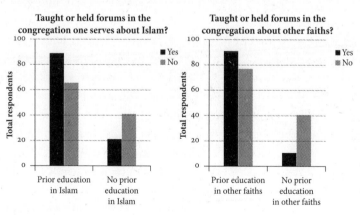

Figures 5 and 6

prior interreligious education and their offer of education to their congregations about other faith traditions. Again, nearly 90 percent of priests who offered educational forums in their congregations about another religion had prior interreligious education in their background, while only a little more than 10 percent had no such prior education. As figure 6 also shows, a lack of education of priests in other faith traditions dramatically decreases the likelihood of their offering classes or forums about other religions to their congregations.

Self-directed efforts by priests to learn about other religions also influence their offering of interreligious education in their congregations. Among the small percentage of priests who have read significant parts of the Qur'an, two-thirds have offered education about Islam to their congregations. In comparison, those who had read only a few verses of the Qur'an or had read none of the Qur'an were less likely to offer any education about Islam in their congregations. Similarly, not reading sacred texts from other religions dramatically reduces the likelihood that clergy will offer their congregations courses or forums about other religions. Just as with the Bible, knowing the texts makes it easier to offer education and exposure to others.

Clergy's prior interreligious learning has a clear, unambiguous impact on their practice of teaching their congregations about other religions. A leader's education in other faiths is almost a prerequisite for education in our parishes about other religions. Exposure through content-rich courses, self-directed reading of sacred texts, conversation with members and leaders of other faiths, and travel that requires direct engagement with different religions helps Christian clergy understand more about other religions and, arguably, more about their own tradition of faith—and sets them up to be teachers who can help other Christians expand their own understanding of others and of themselves. However, even with clergy who have not experienced any interreligious learning, it is still possible to engage their congregations—and themselves—in some interreligious learning by inviting ordained or lay leaders from other faiths to offer some instruction and discussion. Among priests responding to the survey, prior interreligious education made no notable difference in whether or not they invited clergy or lay leaders from other religions to come to their congregations and teach.

While only half of the seminary's alumni priests reported that they had offered some form of interreligious instruction in their congregations, and only a bit more than one-third reported more active interaction and partnership with other faith leaders and their communities, more than three-quarters of them were mildly to strongly in favor of interfaith education— either to begin offering it or to expand on what had already been offered. These respondents expressed desire not only for more forums and speakers, but also for direct involvement by their congregations with other faith communities in programs such as joint community worship services, shared meals, joint outreach projects, visits to other houses of worship, and discussions.

These kinds of intentional interreligious interactions and partnerships are also influenced by an ordained Christian leader's prior interreligious learning—but only indirectly, as channeled first through his or her efforts in interreligious educational instruction. The prior education in other faiths among those responding to the survey increases the likelihood of interreligious interaction *through their interreligious educational efforts,* which can create ripple effects that lead to increased interreligious partnership. But, to return to a fundamental question raised by the priests who do not offer such interreligious instruction or seek such partnerships: What does this have to do with Christian mission and ministry? The question deserves a more fulsome answer.

RESPECTFUL INTERFAITH RELATIONS AND
EVANGELISTIC PUBLIC IDENTITY

Pope John Paul II's encyclical *Redemptoris Missio* states clearly that "in the light of the economy of salvation, the Church sees no conflict between proclaiming Christ and engaging in inter-religious dialogue."[6] Interfaith relations and evangelistic witness can be said to exist in creative tension with each other. As I have previously asserted, conversion is not the point of evangelism. Conversion is God's business.[7] And so, proselytizing becomes an intrusion on God's work, an untrusting and manipulative pressured effort to secure the "end game" of conversion. This is not true evangelism. True evangelism, the proclaiming of God's good news in both word and deed, is a spiritual practice for the Christian that emerges from gratitude and wonder for God's abundant love, resulting in an attunement to God's presence and work in the lives of others and in a ready eagerness to speak of God's goodness. Listening is the foundation of speaking God's good news. We enter relationship not with an "end game" in mind but with an eagerness to hear how God is present and at work in others, and with the courage and willingness to name the holy we have seen in others' lives in our own native language as Christians. This is part of what it means to inhabit our own religious identity while also listening and encountering others whose religious identities are different.

In the survey, we asked specifically, "Have you provided training or instruction for your parishioners in practices of everyday evangelistic discourse and faith stories?" Results reveal that only a little more than half (55 percent) of alumni priests of this seminary participating in the survey attempt to train or instruct people in their congregations in everyday evangelism. Furthermore, among these priests, evangelism and interreligious education are connected. As figure 7 clearly reveals, priests who offered instruction in evangelism in their congregations were somewhat more likely to offer courses or forums about other faiths (they were also more likely to invite speakers from other faith traditions). But priests who offered no instruction about evangelism were also much less likely to offer any instruction about other faiths. The absence of instruction about other faiths and about evangelism may signal a more general problem: lack of motivation on the part of some priests. In contrast, those clergy who offered training in evangelism had studied the Qur'an more intently and were more likely to have taken courses themselves in other religions—signals of deeper intrinsic motivation for learning to live and lead in a multifaith world.

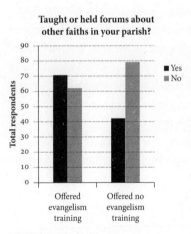

Figure 7

Christian mission and ministry to people of other faiths involves a complex process of listening, learning, identity formation, and evangelistic witness. With only 55 percent of Episcopal priests providing instruction or training in practices of everyday evangelistic discourse and sharing faith stories, only 50 percent offering interreligious instruction, and only 25 percent providing both levels of instruction, it is clear that this is an area needing great attention in the church.

POINTS OF THEOLOGICAL SIMILARITY AND DIFFERENCE

The stronger the emphasis on absolute difference, the more likely there will be barriers erected to others—psychological, physical, and economic. One need only recall the barriers in some American communities to construction of mosques, as well as economic and physical barriers between different religious communities around the globe. A better approach is to name and discuss points of relative similarity and difference, across a range of issues. In our survey, using a scale from most different (1) to most similar (4), we asked specifically about the degree of similarity or difference between Islam and Christianity with regard to a series of different beliefs, values, and practices. The responses, examined collectively (as presented in figure 8 below), create a beginning map for interreligious conversation between Christians and Muslims—at least from the perspective of Episcopal Church leaders.

The seminary's alumni priests indicated more similarity than difference between Islam and Christianity in the role of personal spiritual practice (66 percent rated this very or somewhat similar), ethics and morality (64 percent), and the purpose of communal prayer and ritual (63 percent). Half of the priests also saw more similarity than difference between Muslim and Christian perspectives about the nature of God and about war and violence. In contrast, priests saw the greatest differences between Islam and Christianity to be the two faiths' teachings about the role of women (61 percent rated them very or somewhat different), about sin and redemption (52 percent rated them different), and about eschatology and time (50 percent rated as different). Views about the relationship of religion to science and modernity, about death and the afterlife, and about sources of religious authority were also seen by priests as more different than similar between the two religions. Two themes rated equally by priests as similar and different were the two religions' views of human nature and destiny, and of the role and interpretation of sacred text in religious practice. Overall, this pattern of ratings coincides with lay leaders' ratings.

From these survey results might come an emerging road

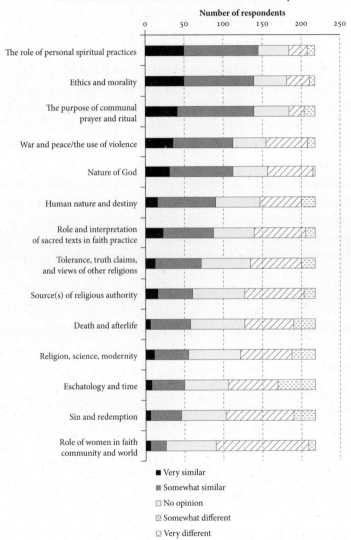

Episcopal priests' ratings of theological
similarities and differences between Islam and Christianity

Figure 8

map for effective interreligious instruction, conversation, and partnership. Beginning with points of similarity, it is possible to foster deep discussion and conversation about morality and ethics, spiritual practices in the daily lives of individuals, and the power and influence of communal prayer and worship. There is rich material to explore about how each religion has understood war, peace, and violence. Recognizing that there are deeper differences in views of women, modernity, and religious authority, it is possible to seek deeper understanding of the meaning behind these differences.

In the end, I cannot overemphasize the importance of interreligious learning for Christian clergy prior to—and continuing through—their ordained ministry. Education in Islam, and in other faiths as well, directly influences the capacity of priests and pastors to see more points of interreligious similarity. This sense of greater similarity, in turn, increases the likelihood of their offering interreligious instruction in their congregations, and modestly increases their likelihood of forming interfaith partnerships with other communities of faith.

Proximity is an important contributing factor, as is congregational size. In urban and suburban environments, where interreligious encounter is more likely, Christian congregations, particularly mainline Protestant and Catholic congregations, are likely to be larger, with more resources available for supporting more robust interreligious instruction and partnership. But proximity alone, or congregational size alone, is not enough to guarantee healthy interreligious instruction and partnership. Clergy themselves must be supportive of such efforts. Their theological openness to dialogue and collaboration—shaped significantly by their own education in and exposure to other faiths—will open more doors for interreligious relationship, dialogue, mutual sharing of religious identities, and mutual investment in the common good.

QUESTIONS FOR DISCUSSION

1. How close is the nearest faith community that is a different religion from your own congregation? How well do you know people from that faith community? What gets in the way of learning together and partnering together?

2. When have members of your congregation learned about and explored some of the core teachings, spiritual practices, and history of another religion?

3. What is the relationship between proclamation of your own faith and deep interest in another person's faith?

4. What do you see as important similarities and differences between Islam and Christianity and how can you explore those similarities and differences between Muslims and Christians more fully and respectfully?

5. How do your religious leaders encourage or discourage deeper learning about other religions, your religion, and evangelism? How do you encourage or discourage your religious leaders in engaging these topics in their teaching and ministry efforts?

FURTHER STEPS

1. Read some scriptures from other faith traditions—not just a few verses, but undertake deep study with commentaries. Bring your insights and questions back to your own religion as you return to reading your own scriptures more deeply. Do this with other people. And ask questions!

2. Talk to some people from other faith traditions. Ask them what they treasure most from their religions and be prepared to tell them what you treasure most from your religion.

3. The Interfaith Youth Core's (www.ifyc.org) idea of interfaith action followed by shared reflection is a great idea. See if you can find a common cause for engaging together as different faith communities in public service and then gather to

talk with each other about how your faith shapes and motivates your public service.

4. Ask your religious leaders to join an interfaith association or effort, to meet and talk with people from other religions, and to continue learning about other faiths. Support your religious leaders' continuing interfaith learning and engagement by helping to make space in their schedules.

NOTES

This chapter is a revision and expansion of the article by D. Gortner, K. Wood, and B. Hawkins et al., "Alumni Survey: How Do Episcopal Parishes Relate to Other Faiths—Especially Islam?" *Virginia Theological Seminary Journal* (2013): 57–67.

1. The survey was conducted through the Office of Institutional Advancement under the co-direction of David Gortner, Katherine Wood, and Barney Hawkins and funded through part of a generous grant from the Henry Luce Foundation.

2. Recent surveys conducted among recently ordained clergy across mainline denominations reveal similar demographic patterns (see David Gortner, Alvin Johnson, and Anne Burruss, "Looking Back on What Has Shaped Us: A Summary of Responses from Transition into Ministry Program Participants" [Alexandria, VA: Virginia Theological Seminary, June 2011], http://into-action.net/wp-content/uploads/2013/10/Report-1-Looking-Back-on-What-Has-Shaped-Us.pdf, 3, for a demographic summary of recently ordained mainline clergy, and David Gortner et al., "Looking at Where We Are Today: A Summary of Responses from Transition into Ministry Program Participants" [Alexandria, VA: Virginia Theological Seminary, December 2012], http://into-action.net/wp-content/uploads/2013/10/Report-3-Looking-at-Where-We-Are-Today.pdf, 6, for a startling summary of racial composition of mainline congregations across four studies).

3. The same pattern held when we included all respondents (lay leaders, retired clergy, and unidentified respondents), but was fur-

ther magnified: 67 percent indicated prior education about Islam, 46 percent had offered some education about Islam in their congregations, and 36 percent had successfully partnered with congregations of other faiths.

4. David A. Roozen, "American Congregations Reach Out to Other Faith Traditions: A Decade of Change, 2000–2010" (Hartford, CT: Hartford Institute for Religion Research, 2011), http://faithcom munitiestoday.org/sites/default/files/American_Congregations_ Reach_Out.pdf.

5. Resolution A035, *Commit to Continued Religious Engagement,* 77th General Convention of The Episcopal Church, July 2012.

6. Pope John Paul II, *Redemptoris Missio* (55), *Libreria Editrice Vaticana,* 1990.

7. David Gortner, *Transforming Evangelism* (New York: Church Publishing, 2007).

4

INTERFAITH WORK AND WITNESS
Stories from East Africa and Northern Virginia
~

Claire Haymes and Hartley Wensing

TOGETHER IN DODOMA AND ALEXANDRIA

> It is my wish that this conference becomes a vehicle for us, as religious leaders, to lead us to a deeper understanding of one another. So that as we leave here, we can share the truth with our fellow believers. (Archbishop Jacob Chimeledya, Tanzania)

> We all come from the same God—he intended us to live as a family and interfaith work helps us to live into that. (Rev. Collins Asonye, Rector, Meade Memorial Episcopal Church)

The desires of our hearts are not so different, however many miles apart we may live. These statements are just two of the many sentiments to emerge from two interfaith conferences convened by the Center for Anglican Communion Studies at Virginia Theological Seminary together with partner institutions during 2014: one on-campus in Northern Virginia, one in Dodoma, Tanzania. This chapter seeks to share stories and reflections from these conferences and to begin to identify implications for how others might be encouraged to get involved in local and international conversations. In both instances, we sought to explore interfaith relationships, understandings, and practices of reconciliation between Muslim and Christian communities.[1]

Under the title "Our Selves, Our Faiths, Our World—Questions of Identity in a Changing World," more than sixty faith leaders from Tanzania, Kenya, Malawi, South Africa, and the United States gathered for four days of intensive dialogue, reflection, and relationship building in Dodoma, Tanzania, in partnership with Msalato Theological College, St. Johns University, from June 23–27, 2014. In the United States, twelve local Muslim and Christian scholars and leaders gathered on the campus of Virginia Theological Seminary for "Faithful Neighbors, Transforming Attitudes," two days (November 3–4, 2014) of small-group dialogue on interfaith and intercultural community attitudes and transformative vision and practices. Though the Tanzanian conference gathered people across vast national and geographic boundaries and the Northern Virginia event convened neighbors living in closer physical proximity, both events featured participants from communities in which Muslims and Christians have faced tensions and conflicts in their lives together but where the hope and intention is for reconciliation and shared action.

As members of the planning teams for both conferences,[2] we seek to reflect on these stories and to share some of the reflections of participants involved. We hope thereby that we and our readers can take from these reflections lessons and practices that can be useful, inspirational, or instructional for similar efforts in the future.

WHERE DID WE BEGIN?

Tanzania

Virginia Theological Seminary enjoys special ties with a number of clergy at all levels of church leadership in Tanzania. It was essentially these relationships which allowed us to presume to gather alumni and their networks together with Muslim counterparts in 2010 to explore their faith traditions. Remembered fondly, that gathering suggested a framework for the June 2014 Christian-Muslim conference, but in this second instance we increased the size of the conference and insisted on parity between the two faiths. By spurring participants to reach out to their counterparts locally, the result was a gathering of Christian and Muslim leaders, students, activists, parish priests, imams, and civil-society advocates from across East Africa. All participants took time to reflect together in deep conversation and connection for the purpose of renewing their resolve to peace building, solidarity, mutual understanding, and joint action in their own communities across religious lines and within their own religious communities.

Since the 2010 gathering, the threat and incidents of sectarian violence had increased worldwide. East African people of faith, though living in multifaith societies as the norm, seemed to be feeling a little more pressured and vulnerable. An important part of our process was to encourage participants to invite a geographically connected counterpart to attend alongside them. It was important that the faith counterpart in each case was a partner, existing or potential, in their context, not simply a random Christian or Muslim friend or associate. The conference title "Our Selves, Our Faiths, and Our World—Questions of Identity in a Changing World" already addressed the vulnerability that many feel around practicing faith in an uncertain context today.

Thus, friends and strangers were traveling together into an unknown setting. Courage was required from all in journeying in this way and in exploring new relationships. Refreshment and renewal were certainly anticipated, but so were challenge and difference. In all instances the connection between retreat and return was important: the conference as a safe place of retreat and reflection and the home context where challenges would be met together on their return.

United States

Courage too was needed and in evidence as faithful neighbors gathered at Virginia Theological Seminary for a two-day dialogue among individuals of differing faith backgrounds, some of whom knew each other but many of whom did not.

The idea for this gathering was originally sparked by a Luce-funded research paper by David T. Gortner, Katherine Wood, and Barney J. Hawkins on Episcopal clergy, their preparation for interfaith work, and the factors supporting and limiting their cross-faith engagement.[3] As a follow-up to this research, we wanted to reflect with Episcopal congregations and their interfaith counterparts on how the research lessons looked and felt in practice. Did the findings resonate with their lived realities and if not, what other factors inspired their shared dialogue and action? What factors set up roadblocks to common understanding? Also, how did this research with Episcopal clergy compare with findings from similar research on mosques and imams in the United States? What factors in the contexts of mosques, those that pray there, and the preparation of their leaders have been found to support or limit interfaith dialogue? What deep understandings of interfaith work in a local context could we and the participants gain from spending two days talking, praying, and sharing meals with each other? We also hoped our time together could help us broaden our understanding of the role of intercultural relationships and understandings in our work together. In the pluralistic society in which we live how do we, and how can we, engage and reflect across cultures toward common understanding and action? How does cultural diversity provide challenges and opportunities to faith formation and to resource sharing across faith lines?

Finally, following the Dodoma conference in June 2014 we were interested in exploring how that experience and the lessons we learned could contribute to a similar gathering in the United States. The importance of faith counterparts, the building of safe and respectful space for coming together, and time spent building relationships were all factors that proved critical in Dodoma. How would they play out in our own backyard?

Shared Process

Tanzania

The planning committee was comprised of the Msalato leadership (Principal the Rev. Canon Moses Matonya, Acting Principal Dr. Joshua Rutere), Center for Anglican Communion Studies leadership (the Rev. Dr. Robert Heaney, Claire Haymes), and the the Rev. Canon Chris Ahrends, an expert communicator and facilitator, who is diocesan missioner from the Diocese of Saldanha Bay in South Africa. Through e-mail, Skype, and much prayer, an agenda for three full days came together. In all of the deliberations around time, space, and logistics, it was key to be creating a community of trust. From the beginning, we were intentional about the protection of time for each different kind of interaction—plenary presentation, full-group question and answer, small-group work, corporate prayer, small-group prayer, as well as *indaba*[4] group time. Ideally, we might have incorporated participants from the first conference in 2010. Amid all of the logistics of bringing people together, sharing responsibility for building an agenda and for time planning proved to be a significant investment. The intention of building in time for face-to-face interaction with counterparts, as well as time for working as a full group, cost a great deal of effort in advance and required meticulous timekeeping on-site, but it paid off in quality of interaction that endures.

Having a structure in place did not mean we were not open to change, it simply meant we were mindful of the interactions intended, and participants could then be mindful about adhering to that structure or lobbying to depart from it. Indeed, the structure was adapted on-site in response to specific feedback on preferred arrangements for prayer.

The importance of voice cannot be underestimated—ensuring that each participant knows that their voice and their story will be heard, that they will have a chance to speak for themselves. Early on we added Swahili interpretation, which had a huge impact on our schedule, but any losses in time were more than compensated for by ensuring that every person in the room felt their voice was being heard and that their story was being told authentically and fully.

Throughout our conference, Chris Ahrends and participants intoned, "If you want to go quickly, go alone. If you want to go far, go together." This African proverb serves us well in ensuring richness of interaction and sharing. If the intention of our gatherings is to implement relationships and action for the long-term, we cannot go quickly.

It was and is slow and steady work. But people of faith convinced of the need to work together will engage in that slow and steady work. We were highly impressed by the participants' commitment to the *indaba* groups, to the presentation of feedback, to listening to one another.

On the subject of the power of voice, participants regretted not having a role in determining the agenda. It would be interesting to conceive of a process that set a structure but that also ensured participants were empowered to be part of the content-setting within that structure. This criticism came early in the proceedings. In part, the process around producing a Dodoma Statement, a distillation of the sense of all present, went a long way to redressing any disenfranchisement participants may have felt around the agenda. Although an editorial group was appointed, a listening process, drafting on the basis of discussion feedback, reading to the group, and further listening preceded the final work. As a result, the final edited statement, read to the group in English and Swahili, was accepted wholeheartedly as the sense and heart of those present.

The Dodoma Statement[5] is powerful, real, and aspirational. On the day before concluding the statement, all participants went out into the community in an act of public witness to visit a Muslim-run school and orphanage and a Christian university. Touring these two facilities, counterparts walked together, explored together, and took the opportunity to commend the two institutions on their commitment to providing a faith-filled basis for youth and child development in their communities. Christians lauded the focus of the Muslim institution on faith in a child's development, Muslims lauded the focus of the Christian institution on helping young students solidify values for life.

United States

As in Tanzania, in Northern Virginia we invited equal numbers of Christian and Muslim faith leaders—clergy, interfaith scholars, nongovernmental organization leaders, and community activists—and asked each of them to bring a counterpart from another tradition, either Christian or Muslim. Since interfaith work was only in the formative stage for some of the Christian participants, we as organizers assisted in inviting participants as faith counterparts. Zeyneb Sayilgan, Virginia Theological Seminary adjunct professor and Center for Anglican Communion Studies fellow, had relationships with many local Muslim faith leaders who were invited to join the discussion to create a balance in the voices present. We hoped that these new relationships could spark continued interfaith dialogue and endeavored to support the development of that relationship by allowing time for counterparts to speak with each other in pairs before introducing each other to the group. We also built in ample small-group sharing time and generous time for breaks and for meals together so that deeper conversations could occur. The faith-counterpart approach was also evident in our guides for the two days as both Robert Heaney and Zeyneb Sayilgan took turns leading different group conversations.

We also followed the faith-counterpart approach in the presentation of interfaith research on both Christian congregations as well as on American mosques. David Gortner presented the paper "Faithful Christians, Faithful Neighbors: How Do Episcopal Parishes Relate to Other Faiths—Especially Islam?" and Zeyneb Sayilgan summarized the findings of "American Mosque 2011" by Ihsan Bagby. Questions and small-group discussions followed each presentation. The group had rich dialogue on the similarities and differences in how Muslim and Christian faith leaders are prepared for interfaith dialogue, the role of geographic proximity, the need for structures and processes for interaction, the merits of educational approaches versus shared action, and the tensions between dialogue and interaction and evangelism and mission, as well as many other topics. Using research to lay out an "objective" perspective on the status of interfaith training and work in both traditions proved to be a good strategy as it allowed members of the group to step back and reflect on their work while creating a safe space for participants to ask questions of other faith traditions. Participants active in interfaith work were also able to add their practical expertise in areas missing from the research, and this sharing underlined the importance of their grounded knowledge. As conversations moved along, common themes emerged, and participants connected over the painful revelations they had witnessed but also the bright spots of relationships formed while sharing a meal or during joint social action.

In order for such sharing and dialogue to occur, however, we found some other parts of the process to be absolutely critical. We opened and closed the conference with both Muslim and Christian prayer, and we provided ample breaks and culturally appropriate space for prayer time to occur. This allowed participants to bring their whole selves to the room and to the conversation and communicated respect for both religious traditions. With a Christian seminary as the convener, the importance of acknowledging both traditions could not be overestimated. For example, these are the opening prayers led by Zeyneb Sayilgan and Robert Heaney:

> Bismillah ar-Rahman ar-Rahim—In the Name of God, the Most Merciful, the Most Compassionate
>
> Dear God, in the midst of so much turmoil in our world today, we are deeply grateful that you have gathered us at this moment and place. We sincerely seek to learn from each other with humility and mutually enrich each other. We pray that you guide us in our quest and help us to be agents of love, peace and justice.

Blessed are you, Lord, God of all creation, whose
goodness fills our hearts with joy. Blessed are you,
who have brought us together this day to work in
harmony and peace. Strengthen us with your grace
and wisdom for you are God for ever and ever.
Amen.

Asking God to guide us, Robert Heaney introduced the
participants to principles of dialogue that might shape the conversations. "We are here to change," "we are here to listen," and
"we are here to be honest" were three particularly important
principles adopted by participants.[6]

Finally, Heaney, acting as facilitator, asked all participants
to share a personal story with the group along with a token or
artifact to illustrate the story, so that we could bring part of our
personal journeys to the room, not just our ideas and experiences. So, interspersed through the two-day agenda were fun,
meaningful short stories from every participant about some
person, place, event, or time that was significant to them as an
individual. These stories proved to be some of the most memorable pieces of our time together.

While the attention to parity in terms of Muslim and
Christian participants and to experience, prayer, personal stories, and principles of dialogue all helped to ground our time
together, other aspects of the agenda were also important. We
started with a focus on community attitudes as reflected in
the research shared but also in the experiences brought to the
room by the participants. We heard about the varying preparation of faith leaders for interfaith work, the role of diverse
cultural backgrounds, and the challenges of interfaith activities.
We then moved to a focus on transformative practices, asking
participants what experiences or practices have been or could
be transformational for interfaith or intercultural understand-

ing and cooperation. Finally, in a move to a future orientation, participants divided into small groups to create both visions for transformative interfaith and intercultural understanding and cooperation and lists of practical resources that could support and strengthen future work. This journey from current reality in research and practice to the future in terms of vision and resources allowed the group to move from the objective to the reflective and to end with both aspirational and practical resources for the future.

IMPLICATIONS FOR THE FUTURE

Tanzania

God is at work in God's world as the primary agent of change. We, however, too quickly want to intervene to "make things happen." That same impulse is often present when people meet across cultures and across faiths. The temptation to ask about the next conference and "What is Virginia Theological Seminary going to do for us next?" was very real, but these questions were displaced gloriously and effectively as we all moved together into the final phase of intentional resource sharing: naming local resources, networks, tools, and people already extant in the local context and ripe for sharing and increased utilization. This was the time also to break into regional and country groups to ensure that all were familiar with those resources. We did so with the hope and determination to work for interfaith action and reconciliation, and also to ensure that resources did not remain the domain of one jurisdiction or entity, but were available to a whole country's leaders and activists. The Center for Anglican Communion Studies' role at this stage was merely to collate these resources and to provide them to the full group for access and use. The other advantage of this resource sharing was to recognize the networks, tools, expertise, and leadership already inherent among the participants and to dispel any sense that an outside force would be needed before action could begin.

The power of being heard and of having courage to speak was paying off in empowerment to act on participants' return to their home regions. The participants' own words speak most clearly of the benefits of gathering together in honest and committed community over a number of days:

> "I have no fear now."
> "Yes, I will reach out, because in reaching out I get
>   my brother."
> "I expected to meet a new friend of distinct value.
>   Yes, that expectation was met."
> "Now I have capacity to talk to my community."
> "When I go home I will begin!"
> "I learned I can take initiative and not wait for
>   outsiders."
> "Deep and open interaction"
> "We talked freely and friendly"
> "I saw the kindness in the two faiths."

The Center for Anglican Communion Studies has been delighted to receive feedback from all of the regions represented about individual and collective actions that have already followed from these resolves. We plan to check back in with the individual participants regularly to see where they stand on the advocacy and action they had planned and how they are faring.

Archbishop Chimeledya at the opening of the conference called on all participants to move beyond toleration, to explore joint action, and to practice hospitality—in short, to risk and show courage. The relationships built or renewed at the Dodoma conference all involved a degree of risk and courage and inspire us to base our work on long-term relationships that in turn transform us for the glory of God to move beyond mere tolerance into love.

United States

During the last session of the two-day conference, participants broke into small groups and compiled rich lists of resources for interfaith work. Ideas poured forth as participants sought to trade resources and to share what had inspired and catalyzed their work and thinking. From individuals to websites, to books and organizations, the list grew and reflected the rich diversity of the group assembled. The list was compiled and shared with all participants and is reflected in the chapters of this book and in its resources section.

The participants drew on social and religious analysis, modeled a process of listening and conversation, and gathered together the experience and expertise of those involved as encouragement and resource. However, relationships—both newly formed and those strengthened—may be the most lasting implication of the conference. Participants appreciated the time for fellowship, sharing, and reflection; or, as one put it, "Hearing from my peers was soul work." The idea of partnering struck some as a model for action. One participant asked, "How can we experience a living model of partnership?" "Building relationships with people who have love and compassion in their faith" was the key piece for another person. Sharing and personal understanding through stories, pictures, and having supper together were all mentioned as strong pieces of the time together. Creating space and time to develop these relationships and fostering communication and connection across the divides of faith and geography is our call as we move ahead. This group of individuals brought themselves to our gathering and in just two days experienced a glimpse of

the power that can come from crossing boundaries and sharing stories.

It is worth noting that many of these same participants are
now working together to reflect on their shared interfaith experiences for this book. It is our hope that this shared action
inspires further understanding and cooperation in the community so circles of engagement can continue to grow.

CONCLUSION

We share with you excerpts from the Dodoma statement, produced at the end of the conference in Tanzania. As you read it,
remember that almost seventy individuals came together from
across East Africa, from different contexts, with varying degrees
of familiarity with their counterparts and the faith they profess,
and representing a range of age groups, roles and expectations.
They worked cheerfully but determinedly to know one another,
to listen to one another, and then to craft an expression of their
individual resolve that could be embraced by all as a shared
resolve. We learned in both conferences that the work of listening, telling, and truly hearing our respective stories, as well as
identifying resources available to us as people of faith, necessarily spurs us on to action. A statement honed and edited together is a wonderful fruit of those shared deliberations. It also
serves as an instrument of accountability, something to refer
back to when we need reminding of our own commitments to
faith in action.

> We are Muslim and Christian religious leaders,
> scholars, inter-religious workers and peace-build-
> ers. Together, as descendants of Abraham, we be-
> lieve in one creator God who has called us to be
> caretakers of creation, to work for the common
> good and to promote and practice peace.

We have met for four days [June 23–26, 2014]
seeking a deeper understanding of ourselves, our
faith in God and our world. In meeting together
we have listened to each other, represented our
faith communities to one another and declared our
trust in God. We have engaged in deep conversations drawing on our religious heritages towards
resourcing the common challenges we face.

Together we face the ongoing challenges of the
lack of sufficient educational provision and relevant
syllabi; atheism and aggressive secularism; poverty
and materialism; environmental degradation; cor-
ruption and mistrust; misrepresentation of faith
and Holy Scriptures; false teaching and religious
extremism; incitement of religious hatred for political ends; violence and terrorism.

Together we reject all that dehumanizes our
communities. With the help of God we commit
ourselves to continuous dialogue; to develop and
strengthen local and international networks for
mutual understanding and mutual resourcing; to
advocate for ethical and responsible journalism
on the reporting of religious matters; to speak out
against inflammatory preaching or the misrepresentation of another faith and to co-ordinate our
efforts for peace. We commit ourselves to using
our theology, expertise, positions, experience,
relationships and networks to publicly promote
and practice ongoing inter-religious dialogue and
peace.

Speaking after the conference, Robert Heaney reflected: "I
have been struck by the incredible wisdom, experience, and ex-

pertise present at this conference. We must continue to connect and learn from world Anglicanism and the neighbors of Anglicans throughout the world. We have much to learn from our brothers and sisters living as believers in religiously, culturally, historically, and linguistically pluralist contexts."

We pray that by documenting the stories of these two conferences we will inspire similar interfaith gatherings, both on the local level as in Northern Virginia and/or on the international level as in Tanzania, and that the goals of each conference, the approaches used, and the outcomes achieved will be instructive and improved upon in future efforts.

QUESTIONS FOR DISCUSSION

1. Who would you consider a "counterpart" in your community or context? How hard would it be to make that connection though invitation to shared participation or action?

2. Tell of a time when you felt your voice was heard and one where you felt it was not heard. How did you feel in each instance? What made it possible for you to speak?

3. Retreating to a place apart can be renewing. How can the reflections gained in that time be preserved as action and hope on your return?

4. What resources might uniquely be available to people of faith to change the world around them?

5. Sharing a story from your personal journey can spark or foster a new relationship. Can you recall a time when sharing such a story helped you reach across a boundary to another person? Who could you share such a story with now?

6. How does your faith community practice interfaith dialogue—through educational sessions or joint outreach? If you do not engage in interfaith work, what do you think are the roadblocks—fear, lack of comfort with one's own faith or with the other? What else?

FURTHER STEPS

1. If you already have a friend or colleague of another faith, can you suggest a series of regular meetings or check-ins with one another in which you consciously give each other time to speak and time to listen, to practice *indaba* together?

2. Locate a local institution of learning sponsored by a faith different from your own. Can you visit to find out how the underlying faith informs the values imparted at that institution?

3. Collect news stories, preferably local, that illustrate a challenge faced by your community. Can you find a partner of another faith willing to work with you to find a solution?

4. If you already have a connection to an individual or community of another faith, can you extend hospitality and encourage a sharing of stories, perhaps using a favorite object or possession?

NOTES

1. We are indebted to the Luce Foundation for providing funding for both of these conferences under a three-year grant to Virginia Theological Seminary.

2. Full documentation, including a final report with planning team members, Dodoma statement, and participant reflections are available at www.vts.edu/dodoma2014.

3. D. T. Gortner, K. Wood, and B. Hawkins et al., "Alumni Survey: How Do Episcopal Parishes Relate to Other Faiths—Especially Islam?" *Virginia Theological Seminary Journal* (2013): 57–67. This research is summarized by its lead author in the previous chapter.

4. *Indaba* is a concept familiar to many African contexts, denoting a gathering that ensures all are heard and a consensus achieved, to which all participants are then committed. At the Dodoma conference, an *indaba* group was comprised of two Christian-Muslim pairings that met once in the morning and once in the evening each day.

5. www.vts.edu/ftpimages/95/download/download_1352145.pdf.

6. These principles of dialogue were adapted from principles developed by Leonard Swidler, dialogueinstitute.org/dialogue-principles/.

5

INTERFAITH WORK AND WITNESS
Caring for Others
∽

Munira Salim Abdalla and Gay Rahn

From distinct historical and cultural settings, Munira Salim Abdalla and Gay Rahn tell inspiring stories about how they understand care for the most vulnerable in society. Their background, religious commitment, and the needs of refugees have forged a strong bond between the two women and the Christian and Muslim communities in Fredericksburg, Virginia.

MUNIRA SALIM ABDALLA
As a student at the University of Eastern Africa in Kenya, I grew close to the faculty and students, especially Pastor Craig Newborn, with whom I had many long discussions about Christianity and Islam. During Ramadan in my first years as a student, I read the Qur'an cover to cover for the first time in my life. Much to my surprise I discovered that much of what I had taken for granted about my religion was not based on scripture, and that the center of all, my deep love for God, was lacking.

The university had three hundred students, mostly Seventh-day Adventists, and only three Muslims: myself, another woman, and one man. My campus parents (the Millers) were Seventh-day Adventists, and we had many discussions about what loving God means. Living around Christians motivated me to read the Qur'an and to question myself about true love for God. From then I began to understand the Qur'an in different ways.

After moving to the United States, I was blessed to have scholars such as Sheikh Rashid Lamptey, imam and director of Islamic Ummah of Fredericksburg, Virginia, and Hilal Shah, treasurer of Imani Multicultural Center, around me. They clarified that Islam is a "woman-friendly religion." I also understood that I had been brought up in a Kenyan environment in which cultural Islam was the norm. Many cultural practices considered to be un-Islamic over time became intertwined with the true teachings of Islam. I call cultural Islam *hislam*, which is how I characterize the patriarchal understanding overruling some of the normative teachings of the religion. The Islamic rights of a woman are rooted in the Qur'an and especially in Qur'an 4:1, which states, "Reverence the wombs that bore you, for God ever watches over you," and the *sunna*[1] of Prophet Muhammad (peace and blessings be upon him—PBUH)[2] teaches followers to uphold the rights of women. Unfortunately, my Kenyan culture did not adhere to the teachings properly, due to the dominance of patriarchal elements in society. The majority of the people were not literate and simply learned based on imitating others who also might not have understood the Qur'an or the teachings of our Prophet Muhammad (PBUH) properly. The more I studied the Qur'an, the more I understood and the more I began to fall in love with God.

In 2000, I began wearing the *hijab* (women's head covering). This act of worship was self-empowering. The feelings inside me were unfathomable. I started appreciating the wisdom behind the ethical dress code in Islam. Unfortunately, we live in a world that capitalizes on women's bodies and exploits them for commercial goals. We have been desensitized about our bodies, with which we were trusted by our Creator. Muslim women, therefore, feel liberated by dressing modestly and refuse to be abused for advertisement.

Wearing the *hijab* was my turning point toward submitting to the will of God. *Alhamdullilah* (praise be to God)! My love for God continued to grow, and the desire to please God grew as well. I experienced a growing awareness of my own desire to fulfill God's plan for me. In 2006, I embraced my calling to serve God. One day I got a call from an old friend, who said, "I have a job for you." My response was, "Thanks, but I already have a job."

However, agreeing to meet in front of the local Social Security Administration office to discuss the job offer, I met a bus full of African immigrants. These strangers in a strange land were delighted to find someone who not only spoke Kiswahili/ Swahili, but who could look at them and understand what part of Africa they were from. I knew immediately that this is the work I must do and knew deep within that this was God's will. Soon, I replaced my well-paying job with a job as a full-time refugee coordinator for the Catholic Diocese of Arlington, Virginia. Through this work I met religious leaders from outside my tradition that would make such a contribution to the work among refugees. These leaders included Jeannie Anderson and Larry Hahn from Fredericksburg Baptist Church, Gay Rahn and Jim Dannals from St. George's Episcopal Church, and Rabbi Devorah Lynn from Beth Shalom. Without a doubt they are my "angels from God." They helped me submit to God by serving humanity.

Our interfaith experience, love, and respect for one another grew to a communal awareness of the same basic tenet of Abra-

hamic religions, that "serving humanity is serving God." I re-
signed from a six-figure job to take a job in which I could put
my beliefs and practices of Islam into action by working with
those who have been displaced, but little did I know that this
new job was also the beginning of my interfaith work.

Through the years, finding a comfortable spiritual home
in the Muslim community has sometimes been difficult for
me. My openness and inclusiveness toward humanity is often
a source of discomfort for more conservative Muslims. The
lack of knowledge about true Islam is appalling. There is much
Islam being followed other than Islam, meaning cultural Islam
instead of Islam in accordance to the Qur'an and the *sunna* of
Prophet Muhammad (PBUH). The lack of inclusivity according
to the ways of our Prophet's teaching is disheartening to me.
May God continue to guide us all.

Today, our community is blessed to have a new Islamic
center called Islamic Ummah of Fredericksburg with Sheikh
Rashid Lamptey as our imam, who has knowledge of true Islam
that teaches us to care for others, that expects us to love one another, that understands our neighbors are not only the Muslims
around us but forty houses around us, and knows that women
are not property and have rights just like men.

The lack of knowledge about Islam among both Muslims
and Christians is one of the causes of fear, sadness, pain, and
hatred in this world. Islam is a way of life that teaches us to
love, respect, and offer compassion to humanity. It teaches that
we should care for God's creation and that the purpose of our
creation is to worship God. God loves us more than we love
ourselves or one another. Love and caring for others is Islam,
and such love and caring are expected from each and every one
of us.

My growing and expansive understanding of that love
clashes sometimes with an insular Islamic culture. Knowledge

of and love for God led me to create a place for all people, the Imani Multicultural Center, where food and provisions are offered to all who come in need. At the center all people—Muslims, Christians, Jews, and others—can enjoy fellowship in the name of our Creator. America is my stepping stone to heaven, because it is here I found the freedom to live as God calls me to live. "If it can be done—Munira will make sure it *gets* done!" My success comes because of faith, trust, and compassion for all and grows out of my unquestionable faith in the Creator. My multicultural background, fluency in English and Kiswahili, and passion for helping others enables me to empower those in need by helping others build their skills and confidence.

GAY RAHN

Growing up in the Deep South, in Savannah, Georgia, I was at times attuned to the subtle and not-so-subtle ways that skin color determined how people were treated. I learned very early that how much a person was loved and respected was of less importance to society than the color of their skin.

Although I saw many religious and class differences as a child, my childhood also provided me with experiences of tolerance. Many of my friends were Jewish, and Savannah has a long history of tolerance regarding homosexuality. These early experiences prepared my heart for a spiritual awakening in the early 1970s as I worked in outreach at St. Bartholomew's Episcopal Church in Atlanta. In doing the hands-on work of reducing suffering in one of the poorest areas of the city the implications of the Baptismal Covenant of the Book of Common Prayer became personal. It was in Atlanta that I began answering these questions, "Will you seek and serve Christ in all persons, loving your neighbor as yourself? Will you strive for justice and peace among all people, and respect the dignity of every human being?"

Homesick for Savannah, my family returned home, where I discovered snowbirds. Snowbirds, usually older couples traveling between the northern states and Florida, would sometimes find themselves stranded in Savannah because of medical conditions, often leaving the spouse alone and wondering where to stay. With the cooperation of the medical center and my church I began a ministry to care for them. Modeled on a program at Duke University in Durham, North Carolina, and with the help of local churches, we were able to find resources for family members and to provide housing and a caring community to offer emotional and logistical support.

Moving to Memphis to work at Calvary Episcopal Church heightened my awareness of the other. I stepped into a town that had not yet healed from the race riots, protests, and garbage strikes of the '60s and '70s, and the church understood its mission to help bring healing to the city. At Calvary Church my eyes were opened wide to a radical inclusiveness I had never experienced before. The work I encountered in offering hospitality to others was amazing: for example, Calvary's mission and outreach supported and welcomed the first Integrity chapter in the Episcopal Diocese of West Tennessee.[3] Reaching out in love to the homeless, the hungry, and the mentally ill was tremendous. I personally became aware of the lingering wounds of the civil rights era when I organized a sleepover for the youth at the church. It was being held just as the results of the latest mayoral election were being tallied, a very close election between a white man and an African American man. I could feel the fear radiating from parents, concerned that riots would ensue when the results of the election were announced, struggling to let their children stay at the church.

At Calvary Church in Memphis I was part of a church that has as wide a tent as possible for including the historic diversity that characterizes the Episcopal Church. I experienced

firsthand a place working hard and courageously to live out the
Episcopal Church's Baptismal Covenant, a covenant which calls
us to proclaim by word and example the good news of God in
Christ, to seek and serve Christ in all persons, to strive for justice and peace among all people, and to respect the dignity of
every human being. Calvary Church's umbrella became wider
as we worked together to discern what bridges we were called
to build, bridges sometimes too far-reaching for some and not
far-reaching enough for others. It was an exciting time to be a
member of the clergy team working under the leadership of the
Rev. Douglass Bailey. During the height of the AIDS epidemic,
at a time when fear frequently dictated behavior, Calvary clergy
were honored to provide funerals and burials to people who
had died of AIDS with no one else to care for them.

Leaving Memphis and returning closer to home, I accepted
a call to Good Shepherd Church in Jacksonville, Florida. This
was another urban congregation whose doors were opening
wide to an urban neighborhood. In this case, however, the clergy
leadership was facing entrenched resistance from conservative
parishioners, as well as from the bishop. Tensions were high,
and with pushback from hostile parishioners and the bishop,
it was a difficult time. However, there were moments of grace.
While preparing for a Lenten Bible study I contacted the Rev.
Dr. Peter Gomes, of Harvard University, asking for guidance
regarding his book *The Good Book: Reading the Bible with Mind
and Heart*. After offering many helpful suggestions he called
me to tell me that he and his assistant would pray for Good
Shepherd as part of their Lenten practice. In the midst of grief
and discord, there were acts of love and generosity.

Following my years in Jacksonville I accepted a call to St.
Mark's Episcopal Church in Dalton, Georgia, and it was there
that the tragedy of September 11 propelled me into interfaith
work. With very little knowledge of Islam, I reached out to

the local Islamic center and invited them to join my church in prayer. It took repeated calls before a connection barely began to be established. Progress was complicated by the conservative nature of the mosque and by my lack of understanding about Islamic culture. Realizing that we were not going to be able pray together, I suggested a shared meal. That was the tenuous beginning of a long relationship and of friendships developed because of the meals. We shared many meals together either in one of St. Mark's member's homes or in a restaurant owned by one of the mosque's members in Chattanooga, Tennessee. It was very slow work.

I now have been serving at St. George's in Fredericksburg, Virginia, for almost ten years, and it was here that I met Munira. In this setting, as in others, I have learned that in order to be open to friendship, we must be willing to leave our comfort zone. Through years of tutoring, outreach, and shared meals, I have found that the grace is in the relationships formed; the work is simply a catalyst for grace.

CARING TOGETHER FROM AN INTERFAITH PERSPECTIVE

On a Sunday morning in 2006 an African woman with a baby and another small child were dropped off in front of St. George's. The woman's name was Jeanine, and she had recently emigrated from a Burundian refugee camp in Tanzania with the help of Catholic Charities USA. That same morning she had been brought to the local Catholic church, but when she insisted she was Anglican someone brought her to us. She hesitated at the steps of the church but was soon invited inside. Jeanine would be the connection for Munira and myself to forge a relationship between the Episcopal Church and the Muslim community in Fredericksburg. Jeanine was truly a gift from God. With the common goal of settling and healing Jeanine and her family, Munira and I met. Through our friendship and our work together, a connection between the Muslim and Episcopal communities would grow.

It does not surprise us that, when we came together to help Jeanine, we became friends. Together we have learned about the extent of the cultural disconnection and the emotional toll of life in a refugee camp as we and others have worked together to help Jeanine and her family. We began to realize the extent of the psychological effects of trauma the family had endured. We also learned that the Burundian tradition was to never discuss trauma.

Once again grace was present in relationships. A group of women at St. George's formed a sewing group, inviting the women of the Burundian community to join. Slowly the men in the community allowed the women to join the sewing group, and the group shared meals, sewing projects, and language lessons.

After Jeanine had been worshiping at St. George's for a year, she asked to have her children baptized. She attended worship regularly, she participated in pre-baptism classes, and she was prepared. What we were not prepared for was that the word was out in the African community that this was a baptizing Sunday. Our church was filled with parents and children we had never seen before. Thanks be to God, St. George's community welcomed all who wished to be baptized, and they were. For St. George's members, it was the most joyful and memorable baptism in church memory.

During this time, Munira became increasingly aware that the long-term needs of the refugees were going unmet and started the Imani refugee center. Today our work continues, never knowing just where the journey is taking us, but trusting that we are not alone.

It has been ten years since cooperation began among St. George's, the Imani Multicultural Center, and the mosque. The work is slow and a continuing educational process. We continue to learn from each other and work together. As our circle has enlarged, we offer classes for adults and youth to study and discuss basic tenets of our faiths and to get to know one another. Our work together has included public prayers offered in Market Square, a city gathering place, on the anniversary of September 11. We share our stories on local radio shows and continue to hold forums, discussions, and common meals, inviting the community to join us.

The work is slow and takes perseverance; it takes patience to listen to others, to work to understand one another, to build a community of faithful neighbors. A quote from Abbot Leo Von Rudloff, a Benedictine monk, probably says it best: "If we open our hearts, we will also find open hearts—it is always mutual." None of this can be accomplished alone. It has taken the willingness, generosity, and graciousness of all the people and clergy to make our relationships and friendships possible—and lots of cooking and sharing meals with the "other."

Gracie Allen once said: "Don't put a period where God has put a comma." Sometimes one of us feels as though someone has typed a period and we wonder who did it. At times we ourselves can hinder God's work, so it becomes very important that one of us knows when to remind the other to pay attention to Gracie's teaching. Some days we think that we are taking twenty steps forward and then seventy-five steps back. Interfaith work is slow work and deliberate work. Often the temptation is that we do not have enough time. How easy it is to believe that we are too busy to do the work, as Muslims and Christians, as we both have our own congregations, families, and other obligations.

Another discovery has been not to call this work building interfaith relations but interfaith friends. We are reminded what Jesus does for us by inviting us into friendship: "I call you friend, no longer do I call you servant, but friend" (John 15:15).

We discovered that eating together is the easiest and the most fun way to build interfaith friendships. Together we cook and compare and teach and laugh together. Over the years, we have become good friends, and it is easy to let our friendship be our interfaith work. But always the circle needs to be made larger. And creating a life-giving circle takes time.

When spending time with others who are different, different-looking, or from different faiths and cultures, it has become extremely important to remember to examine the identity we are assigning to the other based on where they come from, their neighborhood, and their outside context. When we engage in relationship with others, we are given an opportunity to change; it is not all about the other changing. Sometimes we just need to let things be sometimes. If a meeting is not going well, if our points of view are worlds apart, it is enough to practice being truly present, to really listen, to be willing to change, and to be patient.

We understand that for interfaith friendships to deepen trust is a main ingredient. It can be easy when personalities genuinely click but difficult when for many reasons that instant connection is missing and you find yourself ready to give up. We have discovered that working together to help those in need in our community, taking time for clergy leaders to meet and talk, and planning interfaith community forums are vital ingredients in fostering interfaith relationships. But we also have discovered that just as important is the willingness to be open to the Spirit and, when she speaks, to listen and act, knowing that sometimes time is of the essence, not leaving much time for planning.

And so one last story: the September 1, 2015, prayer service. On August 11, 2015, we learned that Pope Francis had asked Roman Catholic churches worldwide to join him in prayer for the care of God's creation. To be in solidarity with the

Eastern Orthodox Church the prayers would be offered on September 1, the Eastern Orthodox New Year. In wanting to join in solidarity with the Eastern Orthodox and Roman church we quickly pulled together an interfaith prayer service, held at Shiloh Baptist, an African American church established in 1854. Clergy and members from many of Fredericksburg's churches participated, including for the first time our Eastern Orthodox brothers and sisters as well as our local imams and members of the Islamic Center. Our circle became larger as we acknowledged a common concern and prayed and sang together. It is slow work, and it is good work!

CONCLUSION

We are all wiser for the time spent together. We have discovered that we have shared affection for the great prophets Abraham, Moses, and David. We share in the practice of fasting, and we share an emphasis on family, education, and caring for others. Though we share many things we are discovering our many differences; we are not "like-minded" people, so it has become important for us to ask each other questions. To acknowledge that those who disturb and sometimes offend us are loved by God and belong to God, just as we do, is challenging at times. We often set up boundaries and God keeps plowing right through them, inviting us to follow.

We come together as strangers, neighbors, and friends. We do not have to see eye to eye on everything, but we are called by God to respect each other's dignity as human beings, which is what we have in common, and to act with honor among strangers as well as friends. We dare to believe that God makes us a community and not ourselves, and that our differences may be God's best tools for opening us to the truth that is bigger than we are. It takes a world full of friends and strangers to tell us parts of the truth we cannot see.

Questions for Discussion

1. Why are we doing this interfaith work?

2. What are the important considerations when you make plans to pray together as an interfaith group?

3. If you are part of a community of faith, why did you choose that one? If not, what factors would be important in finding a faith community?

4. Where do you see yourself and your community struggling regarding others whose faith is different from yours?

5. Where do you see your community struggling to move beyond the stereotypes we often have of the other?

6. Who has mentored you in your faith?

7. How do you make room for difference in your communities?

8. What are the benefits in talking together about how you differ?

9. What are the stories in the Hebrew Scriptures that you share, and how are your perspectives on these stories different?

10. When has someone who is different been a blessing to you?

11. What gifts can you bring to interfaith work?

12. What do you know about the other's religious beliefs and cultures?

13. Would you ever want to study scripture with others who have different beliefs?

14. What are marks of hospitality for you?

Further Steps

1. If you do not know them already, make a plan to meet clergy of other faiths in your community. Invite them and their members for tea or a meal.

2. Plan an interfaith discussion on each faith's understanding of God or on what loving your neighbor means. Invite the audience to ask questions the last half-hour. Have a moderator.

3. Pay attention to what the leaders of other faiths are doing. For example, why did Pope Francis call for all Catholics to join in the World Day of Prayer for the Care of Creation on September 1, 2015 (www.catholicherald.co.uk/news/2015/08/26/pope-urges-catholics-to-join-orthodox-church-in-world-day-of-prayer/). Or investigate the environmental statement that the Islamic community in the United States has made (www.arcworld.org/faiths.asp?pageID=75).

Notes

1. The term *sunna* refers to the teachings and exemplary life of Prophet Muhammad, which for Muslims is the second authoritative source for leading a pious life after the Qur'an. I refer to the *sunna* as the "walking Qur'an."

2. As an act of respect, it is common among Muslims to ask God to send His peace and blessings upon Prophet Muhammad.

3. Integrity, USA, is a nonprofit organization of lesbian, gay, bisexual, and transgender (LGBT) Episcopalians and straight friends. Founded in 1974 by Dr. Louie Crew in rural Georgia, Integrity has been the leading grassroots voice for the full inclusion of LGBT persons in the Episcopal Church.

6

INTERFAITH WORK AND WITNESS
Muslim-Christian Friendship

❧

Salih Sayilgan and Brandon Turner

INSPIRED TO FRIENDSHIP AND COOPERATION

Salih Sayilgan

One's faith can be a great motivation for interfaith friendship. From the early years of Islam, Muslims have lived in religiously diverse societies. Interfaith friendship and cooperation were organic parts of their communities, although one cannot dismiss the tensions as well. The Qur'an constantly engages with people of other faiths, in particular with Christians. It invites Christians for conversation and draws attention to their traits.[1]

One of my major inspirations for interfaith friendship has been the late Ottoman Muslim theologian Bediuzzaman Said Nursi's (d. 1960) writings. Nursi wrote his magnum opus, the monumental Qur'an commentary *Risale-i Nur* (The Epistle of Light), during a time of increased tensions between Muslims and Christians. Yet he laid out a genuine foundation for interfaith friendship and cooperation. In the early 1900s, Nursi noted that it is important to embrace all expressions of beauty in people regardless of their faiths. He drew attention to a distinction between one's personality and character traits: "A person is loved not for his personhood, but for his character."[2] For him, negative characteristics of Muslims that are not Islamic in their nature do not deserve to be loved. "It is not necessary that every attribute of every Muslim is Muslim; as it is not necessary that every attribute of every non-Muslim is non-Muslim."[3] Nursi does not pay attention to the person per se but rather to specific attributes. In other words, for Nursi, our love for a person should not simply be because that person belongs to a particular religion. Rather, what matters is whether we can relate to the person because of their attributes. Does the person have integrity? Is the person just? Is the person charitable? Is the person compassionate? These are the questions that should be raised as criteria for our love and friendship.

After the declaration of the constitution (II. *Meşrutiyet*) in 1908, Nursi traveled to various parts of the eastern province of the Ottoman Empire in order to help people gain a better understanding about the new rules of governance and freedom. Many tribes were concerned about the new amendments, such as the right of an Armenian Christian to become a governor. Nursi believed that religious affiliation should not be considered as a detriment to one's opportunity for leadership in government. As he put it, "The Armenians have certain jobs such as horologer or machinist in this country; likewise, they can become governors. The governors are the paid servants of the people if there is a precise constitution."[4] The principles based on the constitution need to be observed and followed in any case. Again, the issue is not the person and the label one carries but the skills one uses in service for the country and its people.

This is an important criterion that Nursi lays out for interfaith friendship.

Nursi emphasizes that, in the end, such interfaith friendship should lead to action. He urged Muslims and Christians to unite in order to work for social justice and to promote faith in God. Immediately after World War II he stated, "Believers should now unite, not only with their Muslim fellow believers, but with truly religious and pious Christians, disregarding questions of dispute and not arguing over them."[5] Here, Nursi puts forward an important principle for interfaith friendship and cooperation, which is that the focus of the believers should be common concerns rather than differences. Nursi himself displayed a practical example of interfaith partnership and put his words into action. In 1950, he sent a collection of his works to Pope Pius XII in Rome and received in reply, on February 22, 1951, a personal letter of thanks.[6] Nursi also visited the Ecumenical Patriarch Athenagoras in Istanbul in 1953.[7]

Nursi's call for friendship and cooperation with Christians is in line with the Qur'an. Muslim scripture engages with Christians and Jews. The engagements are certainly ambivalent in that the Qur'an is sometimes in agreement with these traditions while also offering its own unique reading of the same narratives. Yet the Qur'an remains deeply dialogical and continues to address its various audiences. Prophet Muhammad's own life also reflects a deep friendship with people of other faiths and cooperation with them.

Perhaps a good example for that friendship is the so-called pact of virtues (*ḥilf al-fuḍūl*) that was launched by the tribal chief Abdullah ibn Judan in pre-Islamic Mecca. Young Muhammad, along with his companion Abu Bakr, were part of this initiative.[8] The pact aimed to end "conflicts and establish a pact of honor and justice that would bind the tribes beyond alliances based merely on tribal, political, or commercial interests."[9] This alliance underlined the principles of justice, and the tribes pledged their support for the oppressed regardless of their status and kinship. Referring to this pre-Islamic pact in Mecca long after receiving the first Qur'anic revelation, Muhammad would say, "I was present in Abdullah ibn Judan's house when a pact was concluded, so excellent that I would not exchange my part in it even for a herd of red camels; and if now, in Islam, I was asked to take part in it, I would be glad to accept."[10]

There are many teachings like this one that can be and in fact are an inspiration for Muslims to engage in interfaith friendship and cooperate with non-Muslims for the common good. There is no greater example for Muslims than the Prophet. Muhammad acknowledges and appreciates the pact that was initiated by non-Muslims. He took part in it in order to establish justice in the larger society. During his prophetic career Muhammad did not hesitate to state that he would still be part of such a pact if there were a similar initiative during his time.

Another example from the Prophet's life comes during the formative time of the Islamic community when Muslims faced persecution. When the oppressive situation in Mecca become unbearable the Prophet suggested, "If you went to the land of the Abyssinians [present-day Ethiopia], you would find there a king under whose command nobody suffers injustice. It is the land of sincerity in religion. You would remain there until God delivered you from what you suffer at present."[11] Here the Prophet was referring to no one other than the Christian king of Abyssinia, the Negus, who was known for being just and fair to his people. A group of men and women immigrated to Abyssinia as refugees upon the Prophet's suggestion. The Meccan leadership sent a delegation to the Negus in order to convince him not to grant Muslims asylum in his land. He declined their demand, and Muslims stayed in Abyssinia for about fifteen years. They enjoyed the Christian king's justice and fairness.[12] These Muslims eventually returned to Medina once the situation changed in their favor. In this classical story from the history of Islam, we see not only interfaith friendship and cooperation, but also an example of trust between Muslims and Christians.

There are also numerous cases of theological engagements. One is the visit of a Christian delegation from Najran, a city in the southwest of today's Saudi Arabia. This group visited the Prophet in Medina and asked him many questions while sharing their own theological insights. After this conversation, the delegation declined the Prophet's invitation to accept Islam. Before the two groups parted amicably, the Christian guests asked for permission to pray in the main mosque. The Prophet welcomed this request, and the Christian delegation prayed.[13] Due to these positive collaborations between Muslims and Christians in the first century of Islam, historian Fred Donner even argued that Islam was initially an ecumenical movement.[14]

In light of the Prophetic example, there is much that can motivate and inspire Muslims for interfaith friendship and cooperation. We shall highlight just some of them:

1. Today the vast majority of our global population is affiliated with various faiths.[15] There are many conflicts in which religion is directly or indirectly involved. Muslims engaging with people of different faiths will have a better understanding of their fellow human beings. Many studies have shown that constructive encounters and friendships decrease prejudice and hostilities and may lead to a more peaceful world. America's patchwork society truly resembles a little globe in terms of its religious diversity. Thus, interfaith friendship and cooperation can foster better relationships.

2. Muslims are a minority in America, making up about 1 percent of the population. However, there are many negative stereotypes about Muslims. According to a survey that explored the U.S. public's view of various religions, Muslims were rated the lowest in regard to their public image.[16] In the research, atheists stand in higher favor than Muslims and are seen in a more positive light by Christian denominations and other religious communities.[17] The survey also revealed what has been stated earlier: Americans who encounter at least one Muslim in their lives have fewer biases against Islam. Gallup's research notes that "53 percent of those Americans who say they hold no prejudice toward Muslims say they know someone who practices Islam."[18] Considering these positive outcomes of dialogue, it is vital for Muslims to be proactive and part of interfaith friendship circles.

3. Although much progress has been made in interfaith dialogue, there are still many issues that need to be tackled in local communities and around the globe. The reality of violence, poverty, homelessness, environmental problems, excessive materialism, and injustice is still all too prevalent. The gap between the rich and the poor is rapidly widening.[19] More than a billion people still live in extreme poverty. According to UNICEF, every 3.6 seconds one person dies because of starvation, and usually this person is a child under the age of five.[20] The national poverty rate is rising in America. Each year more than 3.5 million experience homelessness in this country.[21] The Economic Research Service of the United States Department of Agriculture's (USDA) report released in September 2013 states that

"49 million people in the United States are living in food-insecure households, 15.9 million of whom are children."[22] Through interfaith friendship and cooperation, Muslims and Christians can better tackle these issues.

Brandon Turner

My commitment to pursue interfaith friendship can be traced to three separate occurrences in my life. The first occurrence came when I met a professor during my freshman year of college in a required introduction to New Testament course. On his door, my professor had a famous quote from the religion scholar Max Müller which stated that "he [sic] who knows one, knows none."[23] My professor would often remark that if we wanted to become a faithful practitioner of our own religion, we must first become a great student of all religions and, most importantly, of religious people. Echoing the sentiments of Müller, my professor would suggest that if religion was nothing more than a collection of religious people, then the only way to understand the collection was to befriend and spend time with the individuals who comprised the collection. As the semester unfolded, however, I realized that I was in trouble. While I had decided a few years earlier that I was going to dedicate my life to the study of religion, I had to sheepishly admit that I did not have any close relationships with people of a different faith. In other words, while I could spout knowledge about Islam, Hinduism, or Buddhism, I had never personally spent time with a Muslim, Hindu, or a Buddhist. According to Müller and my professor, my knowledge of only one really hinted at my knowledge of none.

Luckily, I did not have to wait very long. My roommate, a university soccer player, introduced me a few weeks later to one of his friends who just happened to practice a different faith than I did. The truth be told, my soon-to-be friend practiced a different faith than *everyone* else at our small Christian college. My friend was a Hare Krishna from India, and he was, without a doubt, the most overtly religious person on campus. I still remember that my friend would perform his daily chants and prayers outside—regardless of the weather or circumstances. Many of my fellow Christians on campus used to remark that they wished that they took their own faith as seriously as he took his. Looking back, this was the first time I realized that a religious person could affect and motivate those around them, whether or not they shared a common faith. As my friend and I spent time together, we would sometimes discuss matters of faith, but more often than not we would simply "do life" together. I am convinced that the sharing of the mundane (homework, meals, etc.) taught me just as much—if not more—about faith (his *and* mine) than when we shared our ideas of the sacred. Müller, it seems, was right all along.

The third event that motivated my involvement with interfaith work came a few years ago when I became friends with several Muslims who lived near me. For the first time in my academic journey, my "book studies" about Islam were enriched and strengthened by the "real-life studies" found in friendship. My assumptions were exposed, and my knowledge about Islam quickly deepened. Islam became the religion of individual Muslims (for example, my friends), rather than the religion of "all" Muslims. Individual nuances were highlighted, and I was better able to see the unique threads that comprise the tapestry of Islam. In short, Islam became more real to me because of these friendships. Once again, although I did (and do) discuss matters of spiritual practice and/or theological beliefs with my Muslim friends, the vast majority of our time is spent merely "doing life" together. As we share meals together, grab cups of coffee, or complain about our dissertation struggles, we deepen our friendship. Throughout this process of learning about and spending time with someone of a different faith, our knowledge of our own faiths is also strengthened. This increase of awareness, both of our home and of the other religious tradition, allows us to be better students and, in turn, better teachers. For individuals such as Salih and I who have dedicated our lives to the art of teaching, this increased awareness that comes as a by-product of interfaith friendship is a vital and valuable bonus with real-world benefits. Not only are our individual religious lives strengthened—that is, I'm a better Christian by being friends with Salih—we are both better students (our current status) of and teachers (our ultimate goal) of religion.

In sociological terms, friendships such as Salih's and mine are a perfect example of the concept of *bridging*, a theory developed by American researchers Robert Putnam and David Campbell.[24] According to their research, bridging begins whenever an intimate connection, interaction, or engagement takes place between individuals who belong to different social groups. If you were to picture the two different groups as separate states that occupy different spaces, operate with different rules and assumptions, and so on, the bridge that is formed would be an "interstate" bridge. In today's world, interstate bridging occurs in many different ways that are recognizable to most of us, such as on college campuses or in the job market, when people of different racial, ethnic, or religious backgrounds have the opportunity to interact with one another. Interstate bridging also frequently occurs in the places where we live, whenever a new neighbor comes from a place or a tradition different from the background of the other neighbors. Or, with ever increasing numbers, interstate bridging occurs in marriage. Based on Putnam and Campbell's data, a third of Americans are married (the ultimate bridge) to an individual of a different faith, and almost half of Americans are married to an individual from a different faith tradition (i.e.,

Baptist-Catholic; Sunni-Shiite; etc.). Although not every geographic location in the United States is the same, long gone are the days when Americans only encountered women and men who looked, thought, and believed exactly as they did.

According to Putnam and Campbell's research, whenever an individual from group A bridges with an individual from group B (as with the case of Salih and me), several interesting things tend to occur. First, the individual from group A overwhelmingly raises their "warmth assessment" (a scale measuring favorability ratings) of all other people in group B. In addition, interstate bridging typically causes lowered rates of racism, bigotry, and xenophobia and increased rates of trust, tolerance, and respect among individuals in both groups. Because of this effect, individuals from group A tend to become less likely to judge individuals from group B with "eternal" language or concepts or to view their own religion as uniquely true. In specific terms, an individual from group A who bridges with someone from group B is less likely to believe that group B (as a whole) is destined for hell or eternal damnation or, conversely, that only individuals from group A are destined for paradise or eternal reward. Finally, and most interestingly, individuals who bridge with one group tend to extend the same behavioral and mental adjustments to individuals who come from other, distinctly different groups. In other words, when an individual from group A bridges with someone from group B, the individual from group A typically changes how they think about and/or treat individuals from group B *and* how they think about and/or treat individuals from group C, group D, and so on. Because of this phenomenon, interstate bridging has the potential to change the way individuals see and interact with people from every one of the world's religions.

There is, however, one glaring exception to this trend: Islam.

According to American sociologist Robert Wuthnow, six out of ten Americans favor the suggestion that the U.S. government should collect information about Muslim religious groups in the United States.[25] A 2004 Cornell study found that 47 percent of Americans believe that the government should monitor the Internet activity of all Muslims; that 27 percent think that Muslim Americans should be required to register their whereabouts with the federal government; that 29 percent support the idea that U.S. law enforcement should secretly infiltrate, monitor, or survey American mosques; and that 22 percent think that Muslim Americans should be profiled as potential threats simply based on their being Muslim or Middle Eastern.[26] Wuthnow also found that almost half of Americans chose words such as "fanatical" or "strange" to describe Muslims, while more than half used the word "close-minded."[27] Conversely, only 40 percent of Americans chose the phrase "peace-loving" to describe Islam while even less (31 percent) chose "tolerant" or "appealing" (16 percent). When evangelical Christians were asked whether or not non-Christians could go to heaven, 54 percent of them said yes. When black Protestant Christians were asked the same question, 62 percent said yes. However, when specifically asked about Islam (as in, "Do you think it is possible for Muslims to go to heaven?"), the percentages dropped in both cases to 35 percent (evangelicals) and to 58 percent (black Protestants), which is the lowest percentage among all religion-specific inquiries that ask about Hindus, Buddhists, and so on. In short, the evidence is clear: Americans on the whole remain distrustful, xenophobic, and unwelcoming toward Muslims. Americans are by and large reluctant to form interfaith friendships with Muslims and are, as an extension, reluctant to bridge with Muslims. Scholarly literature is replete with ways these attitudes manifest themselves in the American context.[28]

As my friend Salih pointed out, attitudes such as these are most likely due to the fact that, on the whole, Americans simply do not know or interact (bridge) with Muslims and are therefore unable to form interfaith friendships with them. According to a 2009 Pew study, 74 percent of Americans have had "none," "almost none," or "only a little bit" of exposure to a Muslim, while 65 percent of Americans self-report that they are "very unfamiliar" or "somewhat unfamiliar" with basic Islamic teaching. The problem with this result, as we have seen, is that this lack of interstate bridging and interfaith friendship has the potential to carry with it many of the alarming trends highlighted above. On the positive side, however, just as we have seen that intolerance, misinformation, and discrimination rates drop rapidly among Americans who have developed relationships with Muslims, other studies (e.g., Pew studies in 2009, 2011) have shown that Americans who have increased levels of familiarity of Islam respond in similarly positive ways, regardless of whether or not they have a relationship with a Muslim. To state it more clearly: *Many of the benefits of interstate bridging or interfaith friendship outlined by Putman and Campbell— lower rates of racism, bigotry, and xenophobia; increase rates of trust, tolerance, and respect; decline in the rhetoric of damnation and an increase of comity—can be achieved when non-Muslim individuals simply learn more about Islam.*

In my experience as a teacher, I believe this happens most naturally when informed members of group A speak up for and defend members of group B to their own coreligionists. Of course, a direct connection between people of groups A and B is ideal, but dedicated, informed, and passionate "intrastate bridge-makers" who work from within group A or group B can, and must, do their part as well whenever direct connection is lacking.

Practicing Interfaith Friendship and Cooperation

Salih Sayilgan

Building interfaith cooperation on a foundation of interfaith friendship will be more effective in the long term because genuine interfaith friendship will naturally lead to interfaith cooperation.

Interfaith friendship has been part of my daily life for the past decade. When I was an exchange student at Tartu University in Estonia, I met students from all over the world. Most of my friends on that campus were part of cultures and religions with which I was less familiar. Our differences motivated us to interfaith friendship and conversation. I became eager to explore the Christian tradition from the inside and decided to spend a year at Virginia Theological Seminary. This was a unique endeavor since I was the seminary's first Muslim student. The seminary provided the ideal environment to build friendships with Christians. Again, our differences sparked engaging conversations. Because of the friendships at the seminary I came to understand Islam in a much deeper sense. Challenging and thoughtful questions raised by my seminarian friends would make me think and contemplate certain aspects of Islam. Their friendships helped me to be a better Muslim. Once the friendships became established, we could talk about personal life. This would make our faith more relatable. During my conversations with seminarian friends, they would share their call to priesthood. Among them were former diplomats, lawyers, medical doctors, and artists who worked in Hollywood. Their stories were striking and inspiring. In fact, one of these friends became my best man during my wedding. I am still in touch with most of these friends. Without the things that I learned from them and their friendship, much would be missing in my life. These interfaith relationships led me to co-operate with my fellow seminarians on various occasions. We have been on interfaith study tours together, spoken on panels about global issues, and shared meals.

My friendship with the coauthor of this article is another example. We have been studying together in the same graduate program. Brandon and I often talk about our personal lives, our marriages, and our children. In this way, it has been easier for us to relate to each other's stories and the stories of our faiths. In fact, it is because of such a friendship that we have been working together, including writing this article on interfaith friendship. Friendship and trust have led us to cooperate. This kind of friendship is very curial in religiously diverse communities. With such an approach, no one is a stranger in a society. I am a religious minority at my institution. My friendship with Brandon makes me feel at home, because he is part of the majority.

Brandon Turner

Leaving the realm of the hypothetical for a moment, as a professor of religion with a foot in the Christian church and a foot in the academic study of Islam, I recognize my distinct position as an intrastate promoter of friendship to both sides. I have found that the majority of my Christian coreligionists are largely ignorant of Islam but, because of their trust and care for me, largely willing (and hungry) to listen when I teach about Islam. In a recent community-wide study I gave, "What Does True Islam Look Like?" a middle-aged Christian man blurted out: "I knew that the picture of Islam I saw on my television each night couldn't be all there was. If it was, then there's no way the religion would have lasted so long." Conversely, many of my Muslim friends are willing (and hungry) to hear what Christians actually think or believe about matters of faith. Again, as Putnam and Campbell have pointed out, the ideal situation would have the middle-aged Christian man meet and befriend my Muslim friends (interstate) in the same way that Salih and I have, but intrastate bridge-makers must realize that a variety of factors keep—and may forever keep—some Muslims and Christians separated from one another. To pretend that there are no differences between Islam and Christianity or that fears and hesitations do not exist is foolish. However, in this specific example, real advancements were made by my attempt to be a faithful representative to my Christian friend. As intrastate bridge-makers speak "truth to falsehood" to members within their own religions, real, systemic, and positive change is possible. Being a bridge-builder even among those with whom we share commonalities is never easy, but it is a worthwhile goal as we work and strive toward creating the ultimate bridge of interfaith friendship.

Based on some of the statistics shared in this chapter and on the seemingly ever-increasing tensions between religious groups in America, I am convinced now more than ever that the world needs religious practitioners to seek interfaith friendships and cooperation with people who are a part of a different faith. Specifically, I am convinced that Christians, as members of the religious majority in the United States, should seek out and foster opportunities of bridge-making with Muslims, working to develop interfaith friendships whenever possible. As Putnam and Campbell suggested, knowing the "other" in these ways will naturally soften the hard lines of exclusivism that are so prevalent in some American circles and will combat racism, bigotry, xenophobia, and other dangerous positions that have no place in the American context. As Müller suggested, knowing the "other" in these ways also allows us to know better our own tradition, a useful skill whenever a Christian must speak the truth in love to fellow Christians about the nature of Islam or another minority religion. In short, interfaith friendship helps the individual in their own religious journey, helps the individual in their knowledge about the religious other, and helps the individual in their role as world citizen. It's a win-win situation.

QUESTIONS FOR DISCUSSION

1. How often do you encounter people of other faiths? Do you have any Muslim or Christian friends? To what extent do you know them? Do you think you share similar personal concerns?

2. Have you encountered "interstate" bridge opportunities before? What about "intrastate" opportunities? What are your feelings/thoughts about the interaction?

3. Discuss the challenges in your faith community. Do you think other faith communities have similar concerns?

4. What are the boundaries of interfaith friendship? What are the boundaries of interstate bridges? How are these boundaries formed?

5. Discuss potential projects that you can realize with people of other faiths in your local community.

6. Discuss potential ways you can help motivated Muslims and Christians to become involved in interfaith friendship and cooperation. How can we become "that" person for them, a person who motivates them to get involved in the difficult, yet rewarding, work?

FURTHER STEPS

1. Start with establishing friendships. Share a meal or a cup of tea or coffee with a Muslim or Christian. Invite them to your house. This will create a comfortable environment for dialogue in the course of time.

2. Instead of differences, first focus on the commonalities and common challenges. Instead of the focus on doctrinal or

theological issues, concentrate on how members of different faiths can collaborate in dealing with social-justice issues in their community. While engaging in a common project, participants will naturally address questions of a theological nature in a respectful way.

3. If you are a religious person, make sure to spend adequate time learning about your own faith tradition. In addition to the obvious spiritual benefits, this will enable you to be able to speak the "right language" as an intrastate bridge-builder to your own coreligionists and as an interstate bridge-builder to those outside your faith tradition. Faith is never lived in isolation; it is a part of a larger tradition which had determined boundaries and language long before we came into existence. Know what your tradition holds near and dear, know what your tradition believes, and know what your tradition rejects. An interreligious bridge built in isolation has the potential to be just as dangerous as a bridge built by an engineer who ignored the laws of physics.

4. If you are fortunate enough to already have interfaith friends in your life, take advantage of them. For the authors of this chapter, the willingness of a friend to serve as a trusted confidant has improved our effectiveness as teachers and has helped strengthen and deepen our own faith journeys. Bounce ideas off each other; ask the hard questions; and share life together. As your friendship grows, your bridge will become stronger.

5. Lastly, and most important, seek opportunities to motivate other people to join you in creating intra- and interstate bridges as you nurture and create interfaith friendship. They need it, you need it, and the world needs it.

NOTES

1. See Qur'an 3:113–115.

2. Said Nursi, *Münâzarat*, in *İlk Dönem Eserleri* (Istanbul: Söz Publications, 2009), 483.

3. Ibid.

4. Said Nursi, *Tarihçe-i Hayat* (Istanbul: Söz Publications, 2009), 108. See also idem, *Münâzarat*, 478.

5. Said Nursi, *Emirdağ Lahikası* (Istanbul: Söz Publications, 2009), 1:265.

6. Ibid., 2:433.

7. Necmeddin Şahiner, *Bilinmeyen Taraflarıyla Bediuzzaman Said Nursi*, 6th ed. (Istanbul: Yeni Asya Publications, 1988), 405.

8. Tariq Ramadan, *In the Footsteps of the Prophet: Lessons from the Life of Muhammad* (Oxford: Oxford University Press, 2007), 22.

9. Ibid., 21.

10. Ibid., 22.

11. Ibid., 59.

12. Ibid., 62.

13. Ibid., 115–16.

14. See Fred Donner, *Muhammad and the Believers* (Cambridge, MA: The Belknap Press, 2010).

15. Pew Research Center, "The Global Religious Landscape," www.pewforum.org/2012/12/18/global-religious-landscape-exec/.

16. Pew Research Center, "How Americans Feel about Religious Groups," www.pewforum.org/2014/07/16/how-americans-feel-about-religious-groups.

17. Ibid.

18. Gallup Research, "Islamophobia: Understanding Anti-Muslim Sentiment in the West," www.gallup.com/poll/157082/islamophobia-understanding-anti-muslim-sentiment-west.aspx.

19. Pew Research Center, "Americans See Growing Gap between Rich and Poor," www.pewresearch.org/fact-tank/2013/12/05/americans-see-growing-gap-between-rich-and-poor.

20. UNICEF, "Eradicate Extreme Poverty and Hunger," www.unicef.org/mdg/poverty.html.

21. For data see www.studentsagainsthunger.org.

22. Feeding America, "Child Food Security—Executive Summary," www.feedingamerica.org/hunger-in-america/our-research/map-the-meal-gap/child-food-insecurity-executive-summary.html.

23. Cf. William H. Swatos, ed., *The Encyclopedia of Religion and Society* (Walnut Creek, CA: AltaMira Press, 1998), 315ff.

24. Robert D. Putnam and David E. Campbell, *American Grace: How Religion Divides and Unites Us* (New York: Simon & Schuster, 2010). See also americangrace.org/home.

25. Robert Wuthnow, *America and the Challenges of Religious Diversity* (Princeton, NJ: Princeton University Press, 2005), 89.

26. See Blaine Friedlander, "Fear Factor: 44 percent of Americans Queried in Cornell National Poll Favor Curtailing Some Liberties for Muslim Americans," *Cornell Chronicle*, 17 December 2004, www.news.cornell.edu/stories/2004/12/44-americans-favor-curtailing-some-muslim-liberties.

27. Wuthnow, *America and the Challenge of Religious Diversity*.

28. To highlight only a few: slightly more than half of U.S. parents (51 percent) would object if their child wanted to marry a Muslim with a good education that came from a good family; 41 percent would object if Muslims wanted to build a mosque in their community; and 38 percent agree to the sentiment that Islam encourages violence more than other religions. See Pew Research Center, *Muslim Americans: Middle Class and Mostly Mainstream* (Washington, DC: Pew Research Center, 2007), www.pewresearch.org/files/old-assets/pdf/muslim-americans.pdf, for more.

7

DIALOGUE AS A WAY
TO KNOW THE OTHER
A Program of the Interfaith Conference of
Metropolitan Washington, DC
~

Katherine Wood and Taalibah Hassan

Dialogue requires one to listen carefully to another. It is not win-or-lose as in a debate. It is not a casual conversation; it is purposeful. One wants to understand the other. In the Washington, DC, metropolitan area the Interfaith Conference (IFC) has strived to engage the community in dialogue. This chapter explores the IFC Washington, DC, signature "'dinner dialogues" as well as how facilitator training for these dialogues awakened one trainee and produced ripple effects throughout the trainee's local community.

DIALOGUE AND DINNER
The IFC was created in 1978, starting with eleven faith communities. Currently, twenty-one faith communities are repre-

sented on its board. Current executive director Rabbi Gerry Serotta stated in an interview, "The goal of IFC is to create a just community through coalition building, education training, advocacy, publishing community resources, holding public events such as concerts, award ceremonies, lectures, and public dialogues."[1] IFC has created resource booklets for educational institutions to use in teaching about religious faiths. IFC collaborates with Interfaith Power and Light to promote environmental stewardship.[2] Each year there is a concert of the music of various faiths. IFC launched Unity Walk, with churches, synagogues, and mosques opening their doors along Connecticut and Massachusetts Avenues offering opportunities to learn about the "other" as a response to the September 11 tragedy. Since 1978, many interfaith dialogues have taken place. In recent years, training people to be dialogue facilitators has taken IFC to a new level of community involvement.

Of the many possible types of interfaith engagement—lectures, forums, shared worship, pulpit exchanges, social activities, joint community-service projects, prayer and study groups, shared social-justice advocacy, and comparative scripture study, among others—the IFC's dinner dialogue program serves as a successful model that can be used or adapted by congregations and other grassroots community groups, especially for persons taking their first steps to get to know the religious "other." The concept of dinner dialogues originated in 2006 with the Amazing Faiths project created by Dr. Jill Carroll, then director of the Boniuk Center for Religious Tolerance at Rice University. Since then, dinner dialogues have been held across the United States and beyond. In the original Amazing Faiths project, participants responded to questions on spiritual topics by drawing cards. By way of contrast, IFC's dinner dialogues use a single, unifying theme for discussion. Building on IFC's long and rich history with interfaith dialogue, the IFC dinner dialogue model was created by program coordinator Ann Delorey, a graduate of Wesley Theological Seminary in Washington, DC, in collaboration with a religiously diverse team of volunteers. It is now the IFC's signature program. Both authors of this article have served as facilitators of IFC dinner dialogues. Here we discuss the purpose, format, process, opportunities, and challenges of IFC dinner dialogues as we have experienced and led them.

The IFC defines interfaith dialogue as an encounter that deepens our understanding, increases our appreciation, and heightens our respect for the religions—their teachings, practices, and institutions—with which we are in conversation. Ann Delorey further describes dialogue as not simply a conversation between friends and colleagues with positive intentions, but as "a more careful exchange in which the participants seek to share and to listen to views and experiences on a deeper level in a safe environment."[3] IFC's dinner dialogues are not opportunities for comparing, analyzing, or constructing theological doctrines, exercises that often involve religious leaders and scholars working with each other in institutional settings. Instead, IFC Dinner Dialogues involve grassroots-level participants in an intimate, home environment. Dinner dialogues serve to enlarge participants' worldviews, correct or prevent misunderstandings, foster new friendships, build community relationships, and deepen participants' appreciation of their own faith as well as the faiths of others. Rather than debating or discussing ideas, participants speak from their hearts and personal experience, sharing aspects of their own stories while interpreting those stories through the lens of their spiritual traditions.

All participants are afforded opportunities to speak and to listen. This process of speaking and listening breaks down barriers, leads to deeper understanding, and connects persons of different faith traditions through shared human experience and a common search for meaning. From a Christian theological standpoint, dialogues are a way to honor the image of God found in every human being (Gen. 1:26–27). From a Muslim standpoint, the Qur'an says: "O humankind! We created you from a single [pair] of a male and female, and made you into nations and tribes, that ye may know each other" (49:13). We come to know the other through sincere dialogue.

The format is simple. Small groups of eight to ten persons from various religious backgrounds (and sometimes none) gather in private homes over a meal, a symbol of hospitality and kindness across traditions. With few exceptions, group members are meeting each other for the first time. Food is provided by the host, who may request that others bring a dish to share. To accommodate any dietary restrictions—religious and/or medical—vegetarian menus are the norm. A trained facilitator guides the discussion around a theme, a relevant reading, and related questions developed by the IFC, following a specified sequence and using a method that welcomes everyone and encourages sharing. The theme is one generally found in all religions; in 2014 it was "Welcoming the Stranger," and in 2015 it was "Human Dignity."[4] Hosts and facilitators, all volunteers, receive orientation and training from IFC.

IFC recruits hosts, facilitators, and dialogue group members through its website, e-newsletter, congregational contacts, and other networks, including previous participants and social media. Approximately one hundred people respond and participate in ten dinners annually. About 60 to 70 percent of respondents are new to the dinner dialogue experience and to interfaith encounters of any kind. Each group's composition is coordinated by IFC staff to help ensure religious diversity. There is no cost to participate, although a free-will offering to the IFC to help defray expenses is invited at the evening's end, when group members also respond to some brief evaluation questions. Participants are also encouraged to take part in future dialogues or to continue meeting on their own to further the conversations and develop new friendships.

The Importance of the Facilitator

Katherine Wood

In my experience, the creation of trust and a safe space for sharing and listening is fundamental to the IFC dinner dialogue program. Crucial to the experience is "a positive communication climate, characterized by respect, inclusiveness and affirmation. We must claim the freedom to be who we are, and we must also extend that freedom to others."[5] Thus, the dialogue process depends in large part on the skills of the facilitator, who encourages supportive, empathic, and open communication styles among participants rather than defensive, manipulative, and/or judgmental ones. Facilitators ask open-ended questions rather than posing yes/no or either/or choices ("How did your religious beliefs help you in that situation?" rather than "Did your religious beliefs help you?").

To foster a safe and positive listening environment, the IFC has established certain ground rules for each dialogue that facilitators explain at the beginning (see below, "Ground Rules for IFC Dinner Dialogues"). Facilitators also encourage participants to keep their minds and hearts open to new ideas and experiences: we learn more from listening than from speaking. No one is there to preach or to convert others. Moreover, no one is expected to speak on behalf of an entire religion or faith community. That would put too much of a burden on the individual, who speaks only from his or her own lived experience. IFC dinner dialogues are focused on weaving bonds of understanding between individuals of different religions, not entire religious communities.

It is important to note that gaining insight and reaching

understanding of another's worldview is not the same as agreeing with it. Dinner dialogues consist of learning more about the
richness and variety of human experience, including how other
human beings perceive and understand the Divine. IFC believes
that "each faith offers values, insights, and useful practices that
can benefit anyone who has the time to explore them. In many
cases, as one realizes how different other faith outlooks are, one
can experience a deeper appreciation of one's own faith. This is
truly a wonderful experience when one's appreciation of his or
her faith is enhanced in a group where people of other faiths are
valued and respected equally. This constitutes a special experience in a diverse society."[6]

Responses to evaluation questions at the end of each IFC
dinner dialogue have been overwhelmingly positive, and most
participants find it gratifying and even joyful to see a stereotype
melt away, to cross a new psychological-spiritual boundary, to
have their worldview enlarged, and to feel their compassion
deepened. One IFC facilitator from a human dignity–themed
dinner dialogue on May 3, 2015, reported that his group included a Chinese student of Taoism who described dignity as
finding one's true voice. A Jewish woman told about her strug-
gle to maintain her mother's dignity as she slipped into demen-
tia. Others at the same dialogue spoke of the loss of dignity to
violence: a student whose church held a counterdemonstration
against the Ku Klux Klan in Memphis; a Jewish participant who
had personal connections to Holocaust survivors; a Coptic
Christian who described feeling degraded as a minority member in Egypt, his country of origin. The evening's host "added a
Passover liturgical reference, a note of compassion even for the
persecutors: to not be overly joyful with the Hebrew liberation,
but to also mourn for the Egyptians who were drowned in pur-
suing the Jewish people through the Red Sea, as they too were
human."[7]

IFC dinner dialogues bring together persons of diverse religious backgrounds in intimate settings on the basis of their common humanity. Among the strengths of the program are IFC's effective format and ground rules, well-trained facilitators, the symbolism of a shared meal, and the exchange of individual faith journeys based on personal experience in an atmosphere of trust. Challenges include (for facilitators) managing the conversation so that all are heard, and (for organizers) ensuring religious diversity in each dialogue group when a majority of those who register come from a single religious tradition (usually Christianity, due to its majority status in the United States).

Significantly, the format does not allow for conversations that ask difficult questions or explore deep differences in theologies or worldviews. While there is an important role for these conversations in fostering interfaith understanding, a dinner dialogue as practiced by the IFC is not the place—nor is it the program's intent—to address areas between faiths where there may be confusion, tension, or conflict. This type of dialogue requires a different kind of facilitator preparation and more experienced participants for whom disagreement does not undermine the process and erode trust. For people new to interfaith dialogue, it can be counterproductive to begin by discussing differences. Instead, establishing a foundation of trust and finding common ground through a shared humanity lays the groundwork for more meaningful and rewarding discussions about differences in the future.

One particular aspect of this model is simultaneously advantageous and disadvantageous: namely, that the dialogues take place in a neutral setting under the leadership of a nondenominational, nonprofit organization. The setting in private homes is welcoming, nonthreatening, and levels the field for the conversation to take place. However, this neutral setting means that participants meet outside of each other's sacred space, without the architecture, symbols, ritual objects, prayer services, and other contextual items that help communicate what a religious tradition is about. Meeting in a home is a different experience from visiting a house of worship, whether or not for a religious service. The latter environment can represent or imply a deeper level of interreligious engagement that may feel enriching for some people and threatening to others. Religious leaders need to exercise their judgment and consider the formative and pastoral needs of their parishioners as they determine how to introduce interfaith conversations to their congregations.

IFC dinner dialogues are an excellent place for those with little or no previous interfaith experience to begin and can serve as a stepping-stone to other forms of interfaith engagement and deeper types of dialogue. Resources have not permitted IFC to research past dialogue participants in order to learn about other interfaith activities the dinner dialogue experience might have fostered. However, some groups have chosen to continue meeting on their own, choosing their own topics for discussion. Rabbi Gerry Serotta, IFC's executive director, hopes that these dialogues will inspire participants to do more in the interfaith arena, such as joint social-action projects and mutual invitations to houses of worship.[8] Based on our experience as facilitators, these dinner dialogues hold strong potential to foster these and similar activities.

In sum, IFC dinner dialogues are designed specifically for grassroots participants and attract many newcomers to interfaith conversations. The IFC model could easily be adapted for use by congregations, local interfaith groups, and civic organizations as long as skilled facilitators are used. Dinner dialogues could be created between followers of multiple religious traditions or between just two or three (e.g., all Abrahamic). They can serve as a springboard for further interfaith activities, including community-action projects that hold special appeal for young people. Above all, they serve as an important reminder that the "other" in his or her essential humanity is part of each of us. Experiences such as these dinner dialogues often lead people to ask, "How can I do more?" One answer to that question is to look for training opportunities.

GOING FURTHER

Taalibah Hassan

"What are you doing the rest of your life? North and south and east and west of your life?"[9] Words from a song reverberated in my mind. I had just retired and was considering my future, open to all possibilities, when the Interfaith Conference of Metropolitan Washington, DC, announced a workshop to train people for grassroots dialogue. The goal was to extend dialogue from the clergy-to-clergy circle to wider congregational communities. A new journey had begun. This is the story of how that training launched me into doing more.

The facilitator training for grassroots dialogue led by Mark Hoelter, IFC's first director of interfaith dialogue, was held in August 2007. The training was intended to equip participants to facilitate dialogue among people from various faith traditions. Forty people were trained. Within this group, eight of us formed a subgroup that gathered each month for a year before going out to lead unknown groups. Each month a different member facilitated the dialogue using one of the questions from a list generated at the first meeting. Protestant, Catholic, Jewish, Muslim, Baha'i and nonaffiliated were represented. As the year unfolded, friendships formed, and we fostered a deeper appreciation of other religions.

In the spring of 2008, IFC called upon all trained facilitators for an event in Annandale, Virginia. Now with more confidence, those of us who had been meeting together facilitated a Muslim/Jewish dialogue featuring *Cities of Light*, a film about Spain during Muslim rule. Small-group discussions followed with prepared questions. Not only were the guests pleased with the program, but the facilitators were gaining experience and confidence.

The Interfaith Communities for Dialogue continues to be an annual event. This group's format is to have three panelists—a Muslim imam, a Christian priest or pastor, and a Jewish rabbi—answer the same question from their faith tradition's perspective, followed by small-group dialogues. At the spring 2015 event, the panelists were Hindu, Sikh, and Buddhist. Panels are good for large audiences as a means to providing information; they do, however, limit audience participation. Separating attendees into smaller groups of six to eight people to dialogue about the topic following the panel discussion allows each person to speak and listen to others. This engagement allows for misinformation to be corrected and for understanding to be fostered among those who attend. The experience is for many the first time they have spoken at length to someone of a different faith. Having trained facilitators bolsters the positive experience for all. Marie Monsen, chair of the Interfaith Communities for Dialogue, says, "When people share their stories, they see people as individuals rather than stereotypes. We are trying to build community by breaking down walls of misinformation and fear. We hope to empower people to stand up to bigotry when they see it."[10]

As the IFC-trained facilitators networked, other venues came to our attention. I was invited to co-facilitate a seven-week dialogue between Wesley Theological Seminary students and Muslims from the Washington area. Many of the seminarians had never spoken to a Muslim. This dialogue led to visits to each other's houses of worship. After one of the evening sessions, two group members, a Christian seminarian and a Muslim, continued their dialogue until midnight. When asked about the value of this experience, Hosein Nahidian, the Muslim, said: "The Wesley dialogue was very special to me. The night I stayed late, something very genuine occurred, there was a genuine desire to come to understand each other. It was a very truthful, honest conversation. The energy was something very honest about how the conversation progressed in pursuit of a deeper understanding."[11]

Another connection led to helping Dr. Zainab Alwani, associate professor of Islamic studies at the Howard University School of Divinity, in her course "Dialogue with Islam in the Modern World." Part of the course was to create an open-ended question for dialogue, to plan, and to facilitate the dialogue between other divinity students and Muslims from the Washington area. I helped coach the class for this event. Besides the Howard students and faculty, Muslim academics, imams, and other Muslims came to the dialogue. The Howard seminarians serving as facilitators practiced being good listeners. A Muslim chaplain, Munira Abdalla (see chap. 5), who attended a Howard dialogue recently, sees "the value of the dialogue as a platform for building relationships. It was a fantastic eye-opener for the seminarians that would enable them to become more inclusive than exclusive when they become pastors."[12]

These invitations to dialogue have created a ripple effect of interfaith understanding, leading the Washington region closer to an inclusive community. Facilitator-training events, such as those offered by the Interfaith Conference of Metropolitan Washington, benefit those who will attend future events under the leadership of training participants and the facilitators themselves. I have found the training to be transformational; today, interfaith dialogue has become my passion. I became increasingly involved as a facilitator, became a collaborative planner of dialogue events, began to organize dialogues in my local community—coaching others in facilitation skills—and now manage local dialogues independent of IFC. The Interfaith Conference of Metropolitan Washington training program was a crystallizing experience for me.

QUESTIONS FOR DISCUSSION

1. How might this dinner dialogue model work in our local religious community? How might it be adapted and implemented?

2. Which other faiths would we want to participate?

3. What are some possible themes we could use as dinner dialogue discussion topics?

4. Where could we have the dialogues? Who might be willing to serve as hosts and facilitators?

5. Where could we turn for appropriate facilitator training?

6. How could we find dialogue participants beyond our own parish?

7. What other local houses of worship, congregations, and/or organizations might we work with?

FURTHER STEPS

1. Form a small working committee of interested individuals that will be expanded to include an equal number of persons from one or more other faiths.

2. Discuss possible answers to questions such as those above.

3. Identify possible sources of participants, hosts, and facilitators.

4. Reach out to leadership of different organizations and initiate conversations about possible collaboration on a dinner dialogue project. Invite representatives of those organizations to join the working committee.

GROUND RULES FOR IFC DINNER DIALOGUES

1. Speak for yourself—not for all other members of a faith tradition.

2. Stay open to learning and growing from others, grounded in the belief that no one person or perspective possesses total and complete knowledge of God, or of the sacred dimension for non-theistic traditions. Speak from your own heart and experience.

3. Agree not to attack another's religion—its beliefs, perspectives, or practices—or the other participants.

4. When answering questions, speak with brevity so that everyone has a chance to participate. No one speaks twice until everyone has had a chance to speak once. It's okay to pass.

5. When someone else is speaking, do not interrupt. Try to listen with full appreciation and acceptance of that person's truth. Accept the offer and share something in return if you are moved to do so.

6. Listen to really hear the other person's truth rather than thinking about whether you agree/disagree with them or how you would respond to the same question.

7. From the outset, look for shared values and perspectives.

—Courtesy Interfaith Conference
of Metropolitan Washington

NOTES

1. Gerry Serotta, personal interview, 7 April 2015.

2. Interfaith Conference of Metropolitan Washington, www.ifcmw. org.

3. Ann Delorey, lecture at Old Presbyterian Meeting House, Alexandria, Virginia, 1 March 2015.

4. Sample questions for 2015: What does your faith tradition or spiritual practice have to say about human dignity? What in your faith

or spirituality helps you to honor the dignity of others? Have you ever been in a situation where it was hard for you to see the human dignity of another person? How did you handle it? Have you ever been in a situation where you felt that someone else did not respect your human dignity? How did you handle it?

5. Ann Delorey, 1 March 2015.

6. Ibid.

7. Zamin Danty, "A Journey to Human Dignity," theomegaforum. blogspot.com/p/past-events.html.

8. Gerry Serotta, personal interview, 7 April 2015.

9. "What Are You Doing the Rest of Your Life?" written by Alan Bergman, Marilyn Bergman, and Michel Legrand.

10. Marie Monsen, personal interview, 31 May 2015.

11. Hosein Nahidian, phone interview, 14 June 2015.

12. Munira Abdalla, phone interview, 19 May 2015.

8

LOCAL DIVERSITY
AND INTERFAITH INITIATIVE
Going Global Hits Home
∿

M. Imad Damaj and William L. Sachs

A New Religious Demographic

No one at the interfaith conference we were attending knew the young woman when she entered the room. But her warm smile and quiet modesty drew friendly introductions. Her command of English was excellent and soon her story began to pour out. As her headscarf told, she was Muslim and had recently arrived in the United States from Iraq. The circumstances were unclear, but she appeared to be educated and wanted to find work and friends. A relocation agency had sponsored her arrival and would assist her for a while. But she was eager to chart her own course and to meet people.

She had come to an interfaith program at a college. Perhaps one hundred people were in attendance; most were Muslim or Christian. They were students and faculty, professional persons, local leaders, and clergy. A broad age range was apparent. As much as the formal presentations, it was a time for introductions and networking. Conversation turned to ideas for further programs and links between local organizations.

The college had begun interfaith work in earnest. Several of its faculty and administration sensed a need on campus and beyond. The student body had become increasingly diverse, and the metropolitan area where they were located had grown in unforeseen ways. Religious and cultural breadth had become apparent in recent years. By the second quarter of the twenty-first century, the city and its environs likely would have no racial or ethnic majority. Christians would remain the religious majority, but they would be subdivided as never before along ethnic as well as theological lines.

The metropolitan area we are describing is the one where we live and work, Richmond, Virginia. It is a daunting area for a young Iraqi woman to gain a toehold. It also seems to be an unlikely place to cite for illustration of local trends in interfaith initiative, but Richmond has become emblematic of several key trends. The first is the movement of unprecedented religious and cultural diversity in every American metropolitan area of notable size. The second is the rise of fluid exchanges between Richmond's faith communities and their counterparts on other continents. As a result we will speak of interfaith initiative and religious realignment in ways that were not possible until the past generation. We will show how distinctions between local and global have decreased. Similarly, barriers between faiths have realigned dramatically.

Change can be viewed as threat, especially when that change is perceived as extensive, but we make two main points derived from our work together. First, global trends, especially religious pluralism, have unprecedented local impact. Individuals are linked globally as never before. Second, people of diverse faiths can work together locally to build common good. Change can encourage cooperation as well as present challenges.

The key to change is demographic. By 2015 there was noticeable diversity in Richmond, located in central Virginia, and the state as a whole. Of course, sheer population growth has been apparent for years. By 2015 the Richmond metropolitan area had more than 1.3 million people, a figure that may reach 1.5 million by 2020, and a figure that has more than tripled since the 1960s. The area has grown and, in recent years, at an increasing pace.

Population growth in greater Richmond and across the state has brought unprecedented cultural and religious diversity. Most noticeable has been the growth of the Hispanic and South Asian populations. But various Asian, Latino, and Middle Eastern groups can also be identified. Census data do not track religious identity, but inferences can be drawn. Clearly new businesses are supporting the Hispanic and South Asian communities. Buddhist observances are noted in the news. There are Sikh and Jain groups. Annual ethnic festivals abound, often with food drawing public interest and proceeds benefiting local faith communities. The extent of cultural diversity, and its religious expression, is clear. "A generation ago there may have been twenty or thirty Hindu families in the region," a young professional woman explains. "My parents knew them all. Now there are too many to count."

The impact of such change upon interfaith initiatives is striking. Many of the people we know in the Richmond area could not have imagined such a prospect even a generation ago. Despite population growth, Richmond's diversity seemed confined to black and white. Of course historic complexity, and pain, surrounded that legacy. All along there were tiny Asian and Arab clusters, and a small Muslim community. A historic Jewish community gained social recognition and influence long ago, singular in this regard. The number of persons from other religions, especially Asian, was tiny at best. But as the twenty-first century began, this pattern was changing.

The demographic shift represents more than growth in numbers. Persons of varied religious and ethnic groups are visible in Richmond's workforce, especially in skilled trades, professions, and education. While an older generation of ethnic and religious leaders from minority groups is visible in civic affairs, the growth of diversity is associated with younger generations. Student populations of area schools and colleges are especially diverse. Clearly some stay in the area upon graduation, drawn by friendships and favorable economic circumstances which may account for the region's population growth.

This pattern of growth featuring religious and cultural diversification is not unique to the Richmond, Virginia, area. To be sure, the state of Virginia has experienced diversification at a rapid pace. Between 2000 and 2011, the Hispanic population of Virginia doubled to more than 600,000, or about 8 percent of the state's population. In Georgia and North Carolina, by comparison, the Hispanic population also doubled, to 900,000 and 800,000 respectively. By 2014 the Hispanic population of 125,000 in Mecklenburg County, the core of Charlotte, North Carolina, represented more than 10 percent of Mecklenburg's one million people.

The growth of the Muslim population cannot be documented so readily, because it is spread across various nationalities. It is clear that there are some American converts to Islam, but more Muslim growth seems attributable to immigration. To further cloud the issue, of the seven million Muslims in the United States, three million or fewer are regular participants in the life of a local mosque. Nevertheless, the growth of Islam is notable, especially in Virginia, Texas, North Carolina, and Florida. Muslims represent 3 percent of the population of Virginia, or more than 250,000 people. In North Carolina the number is perhaps 30,000, but that figure has increased by one-third since 2000. The Islamic Society of Greater Charlotte organized in 1978 and founded Charlotte Islamic Academy in 1998. In Texas, there may be more than 400,000 Muslims, with as many as 60,000 in Houston, which includes eighty mosques and ten Muslim schools.

In the Richmond area, Muslims and Jews each represent 1 to 2 percent of the area's population, or about 20,000 for each faith. There are perhaps six synagogues, eight mosques, and three Hindu temples. There is a Jewish school and a Muslim one, while Jewish and Muslim students also filter into the area's private and public schools. These figures represent growth and diversification. Each mosque is different in its ethnicity, theological bent, and socioeconomic profile. It is also notable that the dynamics among these religious groups reflect those facing Christians and their congregations. Similar concerns about finances, leadership, faith formation, young-adult attrition, and conflict resolution are apparent.

Mosques, synagogues, and temples have also adopted the independence characteristic of many of their Christian counterparts. Muslims are only loosely organized locally and beyond. Participation in regional councils is voluntary, and there is no form of authority to enforce decisions. Muslims act on the basis of local consensus. There are various national Muslim groups that can act in disparate ways while seeking to expand their bases of support. Jews are better organized locally and nationally but retain congregational independence. Religious pluralism has occurred within as well as among faith traditions.

Not only has the population of the United States become larger and more diverse, this change in the composition of the population has spread across the country, notably in the Sun Belt of the Southwest and Southeast. Once smaller and more homogeneous, such cities as Atlanta and Charlotte, Phoenix and Houston, and others embody the new American religious pluralism. This is a decisive shift. Once, cultural and religious diversity were confined to the largest metropolitan areas such as New York, Los Angeles, Chicago, and a few other key cities. It could also be assumed that diversity was an urban more than a suburban fact. Now the growth of religious pluralism has become a feature of every American city and has moved into many suburban areas.

It is also apparent that the old pattern of American "assimilation" has shifted. There is less readiness to diminish the public profile of one's culture and religion than in the past. Being visibly expressive of one's identity is a key characteristic of the new pluralism. People are less intent on "fitting in" or having their religion viewed as a private matter. Young adults especially defy the intention of their parents and grandparents to be absorbed into a larger, homogeneous culture. Instead, they seek to create a distinctive sense of place, a feeling of having a stake in American life while upholding their particular religious identity.

For the majority of people who represent the new pluralism, endorsement of basic American values goes hand in hand with affirming one's faith. Muslims are noted for founding local schools where values derived from their faith and historic patterns of civic participation are taught. Local Islamic centers may have public events that religious and civic leaders attend. Just as American flags fly in churches and synagogues, and sermons may be offered around national observances, so Muslim Americans may cite the compatibility of faith and public life.

Beyond Dialogue

We have found that this new pluralism and the changing public dimensions of religion alter the ways in which interfaith initiatives must proceed. Of course *interfaith* or *interreligious* are newer terms that reflect redefined purpose. Once, cooperation between people of different faiths was described as *ecumenical* relations. *Ecumenism* or the *ecumenical movement* had a dynamic history promoting cooperation among Christians in the twentieth century. But differences among Roman Catholics, Protestants, and Orthodox churches proved considerable. Nevertheless, the ecumenical movement became a series of initiatives to align religious institutions and the traditions they embody. A prominent approach to such alignment has been dialogue, featuring meetings between theologians and leaders of religious institutions to find common ground amid their differences. Denominational judicatories and congregations may have organized local dialogues, but mostly they awaited formal agreements at headquarters.

There were notable achievements. The ideal of Christian cooperation gained tangible expression in the creation of the National Council of Churches and the more extensive World Council of Churches. Like the denominations they represented, these groups became elaborate institutions, though without immediate links to local religious life. They built programs designed to draw people of faith together focused on dialogue. In some cases they took public positions on social issues that could be seen as controversial and politically motivated. But they functioned as hierarchical institutions with little impact on most Christians at the grassroots.

In a sense the ecumenical movement continues. There are formalized dialogues between religions including several involving the Roman Catholic Church, which otherwise has resisted participation in ecumenical organizations. Meetings of theologians and church heads continue where hope for unity is affirmed. But the new pluralism, and a different religious environment, has diminished the ecumenical movement. Now Christians are part of a wide religious spectrum. There is less interest in hierarchical institutions being aligned and more interest in local, practical cooperation. *Ecumenical* has diminished in favor of *interfaith*.

With pluralism, contemporary American religion reveals a shift away from institutions and toward faith community, away from doctrine and toward personal encounter with the sacred. Faith is now distinct from belief. Trust has to be built; authority must arise. Tradition is distinct from institutions. Religious identity is less passed from generation to generation than it is created anew of disparate elements and personal searches. Membership in religious institutions is declining while participation in local congregations is increasing. Many Americans are as charmed by "spirituality" as they are wary of "religion."

The result is that America is both religiously diverse and fluid in defiance of patterns that were presumed for generations. It is not surprising that as many as a quarter of all Americans claim no religious affiliation, yet more than 90 percent of all Americans believe in God or a higher power as they understand it. It is also not surprising that religious leaders in historic institutions are ill-equipped to engage this changed environment.

Local clergy, for example, are trained to speak for a particular institution and its religious tradition. Understandably they give their primary attention to the congregation they serve. The congregation is the base of their leadership role, the place where they gather with family and friends, and the place that provides their income. They focus on the congregation, then include civic and interfaith activities as time permits. Indeed, interfaith participation, beyond an occasional meal or event, can seem like a luxury. There may be abundant interest but little time and few resources for interfaith concerns.

Yet, in the midst of a fluid society, attention to diverse religious convictions may offer a way forward for many congregations. Any hope of increasing participation requires engaging the diversity of the locality. There will be many people on spiritual quests looking for others asking similar questions of religious traditions. There will be needs which can be met by services and events, including public meals, recitals, counseling services, and speakers. Caritas, a coalition of dozens of Richmond congregations, provides shelter and meals to people in need. This example is telling, and so are the conclusions we draw from it. Congregations in metropolitan areas can draw people in needs-based ways. In the process of serving human need, friendships begin and cooperation advances. We have found ourselves working together on various civic projects focused on the common good of all people in our region of central Virginia. In the process, pathways that benefit our various mosques and congregations also appear. This has been our experience in Richmond, and we believe it can be generalized nationally.

COALITIONS AND INITIATIVES, LOCAL AND BEYOND

In part, interfaith initiatives today could be mistaken for the ecumenical movement of the past. There are occasional large international conferences where papers are read and workshops on key topics conducted. Christians, Muslims, and Jews can be found in such forums where the pursuit of understanding advances. Major academic and political figures may speak, lending credence to the gathering. But it has been our experience that inevitably conference-goers speak of life at the grassroots, where social ferment produces the movements that define religious life today. It may be that interfaith understanding is less reliant upon groups of international leaders than upon an occasional lunch group at a downtown café.

It's not clear how one such group began, but a few years ago the authors of this chapter encouraged several clergy and lay leaders to meet for lunch in Richmond, Virginia. They had barely known each other previously. A few had met on civic boards or through social-action coalitions. Several had joined a neighborhood interfaith day. But most were strangers who moved within the bounds of their own confessions. Gradually that began to change.

Without any agenda other than to gather, the group began to consider what they had in common as they ate lunch together. They lived and worked in central Virginia, and that opened a wealth of topics: how children were faring, who knew of a good plumber, how to face an obstreperous church board, the illness of a spouse, work with students at a local university, a new job possibility. No topic was off-limits; all topics fostered a sense of common journey. The group consisted of individuals first and religious representatives second. But with shared, human perspective secured, firm friendship emerged. Then the group could discuss anything. More important, the group could do anything together.

When a noted Muslim academic came to Richmond to speak, he joined the group for dinner at the home of one of its participants. The unlikeliness of the group was apparent, but conversations flowed easily. An imam's wife chatted easily with the Baptist pastor's wife. A rabbi and a local Muslim leader laughed as they shared stories. The pastor and the visiting academic discussed scriptural texts they relished. An Episcopal priest's wife described her daughter's new job to a Presbyterian pastor. There was no formal dialogue, but its goal was attained: understanding and respect became tangible.

By now the periodic lunches were eagerly anticipated. With them came thoughts about where this group might be headed. Should it become an organization? Should the various congregations represented in it create a joint budget and hire a director? The questions were pertinent. Through several op-ed and feature pieces in the local newspaper and a discussion on local television, the group had gained notice. Loosely they were called the "Faith Forum," but this was no more than a designation. The name suggested a group more defined than it actually was.

The question surfaced at a lunch. Perhaps a dozen people were present, the number swelling or contracting each time as personal demands allowed. If all the interested people came, there would be dozens, and a visiting dignitary could draw more. But most times ten or so would come, and they represented the core group. What they concluded would be persuasive for others.

So it was a reasonable question: should the "Faith Forum" become an organization? People at the table honored the query. Their silence bespoke thought; their hesitation foretold the answer. "We've done a lot and there is a lot we can do," a Baptist pastor said. "But we've come this far by simply gathering for a meal together. Let's keep doing that." Heads nodded and smiles appeared. All wanted to preserve what they had found. All feared a turn toward formality. Their informality had fostered joy and creativity simply by being together. Institutionalization would smother what they had. The matter was resolved readily.

Nevertheless the Faith Forum's programs and audience have grown. Dinners in one or another congregation have drawn dozens of people of the Abrahamic faiths. A day trip to Thomas Jefferson's home at Monticello outside Charlottesville, Virginia, drew a small group of leaders and an energetic conversation about the meaning of religious freedom. Lunch at a nearby Afghan restaurant with a leading Jewish scholar was followed by a visit to a new Islamic center. Freedom and pluralism became tangible. Later, when internationally recognized authors spoke locally on religious and interfaith trends, several

Faith Forum members responded on local television and in the newspaper. Our profile grew.

Early in 2015 six participants in the Faith Forum took a further step. They traveled for ten days in Jordan and Israel. The impetus came from a Jordanian interfaith organization seeking an American group for a conference. The six pilgrims included an imam, a rabbi, and four Christians. The experience was gratifying at every turn. Holy places of the three faiths became immediate and personal. The group shared each other's experience of the sacred and found themselves enriched together.

Travel to the Middle East can be anxious given the reality of conflict and extremism. But this group went without incident. Each day brought new examples of hospitality and deepening friendship. As pilgrimage groups often learn, there was a double benefit: the immediate benefit of visiting sacred places brings lasting friendships. Often profound bonds form when people step out of their daily routines to discover new worlds, and so become fellow pilgrims. That is the goal: abstract understanding must become shared journey.

PATTERNS OF RELIGIOUS REALIGNMENT

It should not be surprising that an interfaith group of friends would embark on such a journey. Images of interfaith pilgrimage quickly became central in our minds and in our discussions. Nor should it be surprising that the trip was enjoyable and free of any troubling incident. It will likely not be the last trip: the group returned with fresh energies for collaboration and travel. Talk of various international destinations, all with significance for interfaith understanding, surfaced easily. After their return the group published a newspaper piece about their travels and hosted an interfaith dinner at a Baptist church.

All of the travelers had visited the Middle East previously, within the confines of their own faith traditions. It was not surprising that they were revisiting some of the sites they had seen previously. Nor was it surprising that they knew people in Virginia who also had visited or who had family in the places they came near. The advance of religious and cultural pluralism in Virginia and across the United States does not permit a narrow outlook focused solely on one's immediate environment. It may be too much to speak of "globalization," but the new pluralism compels a broad worldview. The result is a life-giving sense of being connected beyond one's locality.

An international instinct has been apparent among American congregations for centuries. Many local faith communities have legacies of financial support for global mission or for overseas relief efforts. Just as generations of members of congregations have given food and provided meals to poor and homeless people in their own vicinity, so they are accustomed to donating to international projects. An occasional foreign visitor from a project would enliven congregational interest and donations would increase for a season. Less often, someone from the local congregation would volunteer for mission or charitable work overseas. Their family and friends would be praised, and the congregation would follow their work closely. There was the unusual experience of an international link that was personal.

Over the past generation such links have multiplied dramatically. As Robert Wuthnow describes in *Boundless Faith*, American congregations now foster extensive overseas ties and projects. The scale of such initiative is greatly increased, but that is not the only difference from the past. Formerly, mission or relief work was operated by denominational bureaus. The primary relation for congregations was institutional. Personal connections lent a human face but were otherwise incidental. Now, the situation is entirely changed. Overseas initiative is based in congregations which provide resources to select sites in Africa, Latin America, and Asia. Even more, they build relationships with people and places. The effort becomes intensely personal, mutual, and hands-on. Teams of American volunteers visit to work, to build partnership, to deepen friendship, and to discern future possibility together. Medical teams, construction teams, and groups of teachers surface. There also are student groups and disparate groups who seek collaboration with people of faith in a different place.

The theme of such deinstitutionalized initiatives is pilgrimage. These are not simply Americans giving money or technical advice. They do not wish to direct a program from afar. These are people of faith seeking to build bonds of faith across distances that would otherwise divide. In the process difference is apparent. There are differences of culture, economic status, professional training, faith perspective, access to resources, and political stability. Dealing with difference is a primary issue. Many Americans become anxious in unfamiliar circumstances where there are real or imagined risks. But facing risk and difference is integral to the experience of pilgrimage. And through pilgrimage one can find one's faith deepened. Grassroots-to-grassroots connections bring unanticipated benefits to all.

The Benefits We Have Realized

In part the benefits were apparent and tangible. Several people on the interfaith trip from Richmond became interested in supporting and working with an Anglican Church school in Zarqa, Jordan. Zarqa is a blue-collar city with a mostly refugee population. It has been something of a base for extremist sentiment. Most of the school's students are Muslims, and an important aspect of the school's work entails giving opportunities to girls and young women. Collaboration with the school will include periodic visits there from the United States as well as offering needed resources. When one builds international relationships, one develops a capacity to discern together what is needed in a situation and how it can best be delivered.

Discernment requires that each person involved begin to see the world as people who are different see it. For an interfaith group traveling together in the Middle East this becomes obvious. The same or nearby holy places mean different things for different faiths. The most dramatic example is in Jerusalem where the Muslim noble sanctuary, including the Dome of the Rock, is located just above the Western Wall remaining from the ancient temple of the Hebrew people. The proximity of these sacred places is a source of tension and, at times, strife. Less apparent but almost as important, visits to sites where ancient prophets lived, such as the boyhood home of Elijah in Jordan, raise issues of what the three Abrahamic faiths mean by "prophets," a central category for each faith. Learning to see what the person of the other faith sees without feeling threatened is the key to building understanding.

Further, on an international trip, every person has the experience of being a religious minority. In Jordan, Christians are a minority, and there are practically no Jews. In Israel, especially outside the West Bank and east Jerusalem, Jews are a majority and Muslims and Christians a distinct minority. Yet there are sections of Jerusalem where Muslims are strong in numbers and other sections that are Christian enclaves. Of course, nearly three-fourths of the American population is Christian, giving Jews and Muslims a strong sense of being a minority. When a group builds trust, it is able to discuss both how to see each other's holy places and how it feels to be a member of a minority religious group. These benefits accrue from travel together.

The reality of the new pluralism is that difference, and efforts to address difference, are more pressing than ever. The import of difference is magnified by the unprecedented speed and availability of travel and communication. International travel can prompt friendships that are sustained vividly by social media. Common experiences build and common possibilities unfurl. Yet barriers remain to be overcome.

For interfaith initiatives to advance, there must be local leaders who think beyond their own confessions and localities. But doing so is neither abstract nor complex. Life in an interfaith environment must center on attention to basic beliefs and practices. Muslims, Jews, and Christians must live more profoundly into their own beliefs and traditions. Interfaith efforts do not require overlooking difference, but living fully into difference. Understanding and respect do not rest on artificial forms of agreement. They rest on finding ways to work together for the common good because of each faith's unique perspective. We each are accustomed to seeing the world around us in certain ways. Now we must learn to see as others see and to find common good becoming possible.

This is the advantage of our approach to interfaith relations. We are neither remote and institutional, nor strictly independent and congregational. We have built a bond focused on finding the common good in the region where we live. Literally and symbolically we have learned to walk together and, in the process, have formed ties that will not erode. Among us there is much to be affirmed together.

Each of the Abrahamic faiths speaks of "love of God and love of neighbor." Each takes a different path to this affirmation. In practice, this shared emphasis is what matters. In the same metropolitan area people of each faith face common challenges, common opportunities, and common need for direction. When people awaken to shared circumstances, differences need not dominate. Common ground is identified. The global and the local meld. Understanding and cooperation advance, in Richmond, or anywhere else.

Questions for Discussion

1. How has the religious demography of your community changed over the past generation? What religious and ethnic groups are new in your area?

2. With what people of different faiths does your congregation have contact? Is your contact occasional or sustained?

3. After reading this chapter, what do you feel you and your congregation have in common with people of other faiths, especially Muslims and Jews?

4. In your experience what has been the greatest obstacle to interfaith cooperation?

5. In your community and beyond, what could people of different faiths do together to benefit public life?

Further Steps

1. Reach out to a local mosque or synagogue by having lunch or dinner with their leader. Better yet, have a dinner in your congregation for a group of local leaders from different faith communities.

2. Explore the possibility of having a local imam or rabbi speak to your congregation. Their perspective and expertise will enhance your congregation's educational program.

3. Identify a service project that can bring together volunteers from different faith groups in your area. Work together to house and feed people in need.

4. Have an informed speaker, perhaps from a local college, lead a class on the common beliefs and morals of Christianity, Islam, and Judaism.

5. Gather a group of interfaith leaders to visit a place of historical significance in your area. Discuss how this place helped to shape the values and priorities of your community.

Part Three

FAITHFUL NEIGHBORS:
PRACTICES AND PRINCIPLES

9

PRINCIPLES FOR CONSTRUCTIVE
INTERFAITH CONVERSATION
∼

Robert Heaney and Zeyneb Sayilgan

Faithful Neighbors as
Constructive Conversation

In reviewing and summarizing the contributions to the present volume it becomes evident that particular principles of constructive dialogue are at work. These attributes emerge not only from the essays in this book but also from planning conversations for the work of the Center for Anglican Communion Studies, interfaith dialogues, and how we experienced these conversations both in East Africa and Northern Virginia. We have identified seven such practices of constructive conversation: self-discovery, relationships, generosity, difference, power relations, contextualism, and humility. These practices are at work across the chapters of this book and in the witness and work of the contributors.

David Gortner's piece surveying the attitudes of Episcopal

clergy and lay leaders toward interfaith education also directs our attention to an infamous "elephant in the room." For the issues of evangelism and proselytizing for Christians and perhaps *da'wa* for Muslims (invitation and call to Islam) remain contentious. Both Christians and Muslims love their faith and naturally want to share their spiritual treasures with others. Gortner offers a very valuable definition of Christian mission and evangelism for today, which we think could equally be supported by many Muslims.

Islam teaches that conversion is truly God's business, and even the Prophet Muhammad is taught through revelation that only God can guide the hearts of his loved ones to faith: "Indeed, you cannot guide whom you love, but God guides whom He pleases, and He knows best the followers of the right way" (Qur'an 28:56). The Prophet can only live and proclaim the message. "There is no compulsion in religion" (2:256), as the Qur'an maintains.

While conversion as a by-product of interfaith conversation cannot be avoided, it is not the "end game," as Gortner rightly stresses. True evangelism, as he asserts, should be first and foremost about trying to discover the holiness in your fellow beings. It should not be an exercise in seeking to overpower another's faith commitment; rather, evangelism is listening attentively and then confidently sharing your own voice. It is then, he emphasizes, that interfaith relations and evangelism can exist in creative tension with each other. To reiterate, there is nothing wrong in trying to share what you hold most precious—your faith. This only expresses a deep care and compassion towards the Other. Yet such sharing needs to go hand in hand with generous listening.

Claire Haymes and Hartley Wensing skillfully tell the story of two distinct, and yet related, Christian-Muslim events—one in North America and one in East Africa. In both contexts participants entered into a deep time of listening and found their voices as individual believers and together as people of faith. Relationship was central to both ventures. In Tanzania the relationships were both international and local with alumni of Virginia Theological Seminary, graduates of past Center for Anglican Communion Studies interfaith work, and local believers coming together to discuss difference as well as commonality with the purpose of committing to ongoing engagement and action. In Virginia, the relationships were localized, arising from connections the Center had with both Muslim and Christian practitioners in local settings.

A common theme in both contexts was a desire to be builders of peace and leaders for change. That meant participants bringing together their expertise and resources to help each other move forward in deeper and more effective interfaith engagement. This is captured powerfully in the Dodoma Statement: "[A]s descendants of Abraham, we believe in one creator God who has called us to be caretakers of creation, to work for the common good and to promote and practice peace." As people of faith the participants resolved together in partnership to "reject all that dehumanizes our communities." Yet the change was not something that participants sought to do or to achieve beyond the consultations. In truth, the conversations, the testifying, the misunderstandings, the moments of clarity and elucidation, and the sense of emerging community changed everyone. It brought home in a very real sense that it is God who welcomes us into conversation and blesses our conversations.

In their essays, Gay Rahn and Munira Abdalla remind us of one key principle for constructive interfaith conversation. They mention the concept of love. Their love of God and generosity led them to reach out and embrace others, to show hospitality to the stranger, and to challenge social sins such as racism and religious arrogance. Both insist that God's love is expansive and all-inclusive.

With the desire to attain God's love, Rahn and Abdalla dedicated themselves to eradicate humanly constructed barriers and walls of separation. They did not need to go far since religious intolerance and arrogance exist in both Christian and Muslim communities. It comes with no surprise that Jesus and Muhammad (peace be upon them) began their mission in their own social environment. As seen in the reality of Rahn's and Abdalla's lives, often religion becomes the prime reason to exclude other fellow human beings based on race, gender, or religion. While the term *love* is on everyone's lips, Rahn and Abdalla's attitude demonstrates that a believer cannot only pay lip service to this overarching divine theme. A devout person has to act upon it, first by fundamentally internalizing that every being contains the divine spark and is therefore dignified by the Creator. This is regardless of the fact whether such a person denies the existence of God or insists on living a sinful life. It is in this light that we understand a famous Prophetic tradition that states, "If you love your Creator, serve the creation."

While the Qur'an clearly affirms that God loves and also dislikes certain character traits and behavior, this has never meant for Muslims that anyone is excluded from God's love. In fact, Muslim scripture, except in one case, always begins its chapters with the formula "In the Name of God, the Most Merciful, the Most Compassionate." As Muslims and Christians—paying sometimes too much attention to the theological differences which certainly should not be undermined—we need not lose sight of primary commonalities and how to use these resources to alleviate the social suffering around us. What would happen if Rahn and Abdalla spent their precious days reflecting and arguing about the difference in some theological doctrines? As people of faith who are living in very fast and turbulent times, we should be pragmatic and use our time more effectively and wisely. Our traditions are rich enough to join hands in fighting some of the social diseases around us. In Rahn and Abdalla we see a simple but yet profound example of how to accomplish this goal. Their love does not remain on an abstract level but is expressed through many important social-justice activities. If God's love is the seed of this universe, then we as believers have a special responsibility to help spread this love.

Love of God also entails engaging with the diversity of religious traditions present all around us. Such diversity, as the Qur'an affirms, is divinely willed and affirmed: "To each of you We prescribed a law and a method. Had God willed, He would have made you one nation [united in religion], but [He intended] to test you in what He has given you; so race to [all that is] good. To God is your return all together, and He will [then] inform you concerning that over which you used to differ" (Qur'an 5:48).

Salih Sayilgan and Brandon Turner exhibit such love of God as they explore interfaith practices of friendship. The practice of friendship is vital to interfaith engagement, and yet it can be overlooked in favor of what might be thought of as "higher-level" concerns. Sayilgan and Turner's thoughtful piece, however, warns us away from making the error of undervaluing interfaith friendship or of undervaluing time spent reflecting on its nature and value.

Not only do Sayilgan and Turner reflect on their own experiences and practices of interfaith friendship, they also point to the social change that results from such friendships. The openness and skill to build friendships and to act as a bridge across differences results in lower rates of racism, bigotry, and xenophobia. Interfaith friendships in fact create better communities. Where such bridges are built communities benefit from higher rates of trust, tolerance, and respect. Their essay describes an everyday occurrence that can influence social justice, counter atheism, and define the common good and common work toward that good. We all are called to be friends. Sayilgan and Turner provide us with resources to practice friendship across religions as a blessing to ourselves and our communities.

Katherine Wood and Taalibah Hassan explore the benefits of interfaith conversation in the context of hospitality. They ably describe the rationale and method of Interfaith Conference dinner dialogues, noting that the dialogues are a particularly helpful introduction to interfaith engagement. For people talk together and eat together not on the basis of some theological expertise but from the perspective of lived experience. As in any good and constructive interfaith conversation, there is no assumption that one's voice and one's lived experience represent an entire faith tradition. Rather, in conversation one enters into an experience of discovery.

In this very encouraging context for engagement they define dialogue as encounter for deeper understanding and greater respect. The model is replicable and serves the grassroots, and is particularly suited to people with no or little interfaith experience, for they are welcomed into a conversation that is nonthreatening. These lively and enjoyable dinner dialogues undermine stereotypes, deconstruct misinformation and misunderstanding, take away fear, and equip people with the knowledge and voice to stand against bigotry.

William Sachs and Imam Imad Damaj highlight in their piece that the phenomenon of religious pluralism can no longer be ignored and that it has even reached, it seems, every suburban context in North America. The context in the global North is changing, and such religious change also requires a change of attitudes. Engagement with religious diversity is vitally important to help connections between people across the globe become even more apparent. Engagement with the religious other locally can also result in long-lasting positive changes globally. The importance cannot be overestimated. Theologically, believers should feel the obligation to reach out to one another for the common good. In fact, many social and economic grievances could be tackled more effectively if people of faith would unite their intellectual and social forces. Most profoundly, this is done on the grassroots or micro level. Sachs and Damaj rightly argue against certain formalism and institutionalized decrees from the top. Instead, what we witness in our age is personal motivation leading organically to encounters with followers of other faiths.

It doesn't take much for such organic movements to come into existence. In Sachs and Damaj's example, it was a rather humble and simple suggestion for a regular meal which then, over time, resulted in collaborative work, group pilgrimages, and ultimately a joint humanitarian project. What simple yet profound and transformative activities! Often we can be caught up in formalities or think on a macro level, such as gathering five hundred people for an interfaith lecture. Otherwise we think it's not worth the effort. To our mind, it is the quality and sincerity of the encounter, not the quantity of people involved, that creates wide impact.

While engaging with one another, all participants agree not to overlook their differences, but to fully live into their differences. This is probably the most crucial aspect of authentic interfaith work. Some might perceive such difference as a threat and attempt to undermine it. However, it is only when we are confident and expressive about who we are that a constructive conversation takes place. Certainly, this will take time and only occur once mutual trust is established. Yet it is critically important to uphold the integrity of our faith traditions and not to pretend that differences are nonexistent. It is only then that we are hospitable to one another in the most generous way. By welcoming God's creative diversity, neighborly love is fully lived.

What Makes Interfaith Conversation "Constructive"?

The witness of the "faithful neighbors" in this volume points to at least seven aspects we want to highlight as, in part, defining what we call constructive conversation.

First, constructive interfaith conversation is a journey of *self-discovery*. Those who enter into interfaith conversation need not be experts in the faith tradition they represent. This book is not a collection written by experts in interfaith dynamics or dialogue. It is a collection of testimonies of people who have reached out across cultural and religious difference. In the conferences and consultations that the Center for Anglican Communion Studies hosted prior to producing this volume, believers pointed not to some major theological breakthrough but to personal breakthrough. Interfaith conversation transforms people. It has transformed us. This transformation might come about as questions are asked about particular tenets of belief or about particular rituals. Such transformation often results in a deeper understanding of ourselves as adherents and practitioners of faith. We would argue, therefore, that interfaith conversation is not a reductionist exercise but an opportunity for deeper commitment to God. Constructive conversation is not a "watering down" of faith commitment but, on the contrary, a remedy for nominalism and weak imitations of faith unmoored from knowledge and conviction. Constructive interfaith conversation is first and foremost a road to self-discovery, a means to clarity on one's faith journey.

Second, constructive interfaith conversation is *relational*. A cursory look at surveys reveals that most often those people who are strongly opposed or hostile toward another group are those who have had no or little exposure to them. Worse, through the media people gain a "virtual" exposure to the Other often framed by recent atrocities or partisan headlines and analysis. Interfaith conversation transforms such a situation. In the very act of reaching out to a faithful neighbor one is refusing to have one's attitudes defined simply by sensationalist media or sensational events. Rather, one is transformed through relationship, and one's community is transformed through relationship.

Third, constructive interfaith conversation is *generous*. The point of departure cannot be historic or contemporary atrocities carried out in the name of religion. While such brutality cannot be ignored, it is always wise to begin with a generous spirit that seeks the voice and presence of God in the Other. While initiating a conversation, be careful in comparing realities with realities and ideals with ideals. Often, dialogue can be unfair in that we reference the worst examples of another faith and compare them to the other tradition's ideals. We all know very well that each faith community has bad and good representatives. Ideally, we should seek the people who live up to the ideals of that tradition in order to understand the tradition fully. A constructive conversation eschews simple stereotypes and comparisons between, in this case, Islam and Christianity. We fear what we do not know, and often these preconceived notions about a certain group can define our whole attitude. It is therefore essential to be charitable in listening attentively to the conversation partner and not to allow for misconstrued images and opinions to define the dialogue. This point we cannot overemphasize enough.

Fourth, constructive interfaith conversation *affirms difference*. It is vitally important that the differences between faith commitments are honored. Constructive interfaith conversation should preserve the distinct characteristics of each religion, disallowing any moves toward reductionist banality. Undoubtedly, there is common ground between the Christian and Islamic faiths. However, each tradition has something unique to offer and, in that sense, cannot be assumed simply to be the same. This is not the goal of dialogue. If we come out of an encounter fully accepting our difference, then the conversation has been constructive.

Fifth, constructive interfaith conversation *takes account of power relations*. When power relations are not considered, interfaith conversations can take place in less than just ways. For example, imagine a conversation in which, on the Christian side, trained theologians speak and, on the other side, Muslim laypeople, not thoroughly trained in their tradition, speak. This is an unhappy and inhospitable point of departure. The authors in this volume demonstrate that they take account of power relations and seek fairness and balance as they meet as equals. While there is no global rule on whom to engage, a constructive conversation depends upon equality. That equality might be understood in relation to how power is exhibited in regard to class, race, culture, gender, training, and theological conviction.

Sixth, constructive interfaith conversation is *contextual*. Every person of faith comes from a particular social, historical, political, or cultural context. Faith commitment is not lived in a vacuum. Neither Christianity nor Islam is a monolith. For that reason the diversity of faith commitments and the diversity of embodied faith expressions must be kept in view and, where possible, must become part of the conversation. Without this contextual dimension, interfaith conversations can further embed stereotypes instead of overcoming them. That is not to say that contextual conversation need always be deeply complex or undertaken on a grand scale. That the conversation is sustained is more important than whether or not it is carried out at a "high level." Indeed, the truly qualitative encounter often happens in small and regular gatherings. In examples in this book we clearly see that meaningful dialogue in small contexts can have deep impact. With a focus on local context in a neighborhood, a school, or a workplace, transformation takes place and begins to have wider impact. Transforming the microcosm may well change the macrocosm.

Seventh, constructive interfaith conversation is marked by *humility*. While it is important to be aware of how the past informs the present, we recognize that the past need not determine the present. To acknowledge past mistakes and malpractices is to recognize that no one can claim the moral high ground. Such acknowledgment is to move forward, always dependent on the mercy of God with mercy extended to each other.

Conclusion

For a believer, constructive interfaith conversation should be an inherent part of one's personal faith practice. Both of our traditions, Islam and Christianity, consider themselves universal in nature. They are dialogical in nature and have from their very beginnings displayed an active outreach ministry. Adherents of these religions should therefore regard dialogue as intrinsic to their traditions. Such a practice should not be seen as something you only do when you have time. There is a theological imperative to reach out to your fellow human beings in order to express hospitality, increase understanding, and establish mutual trust. There is no denying that much evil can be eradicated if ignorance and xenophobia are challenged. In a world that witnesses so much spiritual and moral decline, coming together with people of other faiths can create much goodness.

Neither Muslims nor Christians can exist in isolation from each other. They need to unite their spiritual and intellectual resources in order to fight common challenges. The rise of materialism, egotism, and aggressive secularism are only a few of the moral threats challenging our communities. We are one human family created with the *imago Dei*, as both Muslims and Christians affirm. To reach out to your Muslim or Christian neighbor is fundamentally to honor God by creating faith alliances. To reach out constructively is to step into a journey of self-discovery, relationship, generosity, and difference, having been enabled to take account of power relations and context in a spirit of humility.

QUESTIONS FOR DISCUSSION

1. Which chapter in this book did you find particularly helpful? Why?

2. How do you imagine "constructive interfaith conversation"?

3. What are the do's and don'ts of a fruitful dialogue?

4. How have you changed as a result of reading this book?

FURTHER STEPS

1. Don't wait for others to approach you to enter an interfaith conversation. Take the initiative. Open your heart and your home and you will find others to join you.

2. Begin some self-study to acquire at least some basic understanding of other religious traditions (see the resource section at the end of this book).

3. Define personal strengths and talents that would be helpful for realizing your interfaith vision.

4. Assess the real possibilities and resources for interfaith conversation in your own locality. Reach out to different communities if you can. Some research on the Internet can be helpful as well. Most religious communities have umbrella organizations overseeing their nationwide religious centers. They can be valuable in finding local contacts.

5. Identify two to four people who would be interested in joining an interfaith project and creating a powerful faith alliance.

6. Begin with a small but qualitative idea as seen in the experiences introduced in this book—an interfaith meal, book club, charity project, lecture, visit to local religious centers, pilgrimage, or study tour. Remember, it does not need to be a big event to be meaningful and transformative.

7. Be patient with the process. Long-term results and benefits need perseverance.

8. Keep a log along your interfaith journey and review later which steps do or do not work.

9. Connect with the Center for Anglican Communion Studies via Facebook and Twitter.

RESOURCES
~

James Stambaugh

PRINT

Bennett, Clinton. *Understanding Christian-Muslim Relations.* London and New York: Continuum, 2008.

Brown Jr., Daniel S., ed. *Interfaith Dialogue in Practice: Christian, Muslim, Jew.* Kansas City: Rockhurst University Press, 2012.

Chapman, Colin Gilbert. *Cross and Crescent: Responding to the Challenge of Islam.* Leicester, England: Inter-Varsity Press, 1996.

Cragg, Kenneth, ed. *Common Prayer: A Muslim-Christian Spiritual Anthology.* Oxford: Oneworld, 1999.

———. *Sandals at the Mosque: Christian Presence amid Islam.* Christian Presence Series. London: SCM, 1959.

Demiri, Lejla, David B. Burrell, and Abdal Hakim Murad. *A Common Word: Texts and Reflections. A Resource for Parishes and Mosques.* Cambridge, England: Muslim Academic Trust, 2011.

Gaston, Ray. *A Heart Broken Open: Radical Faith in an Age of Fear.* Glasgow: Wild Goose Publications, 2009.

Goddard, Hugh. *A History of Christian-Muslim Relations.* Edinburgh: Edinburgh University Press, 2000.

Lamb, Christopher, and Rowan Williams. *A Policy of Hope: Kenneth Cragg and Islam*. Revised and updated. London: Melisende, 2014.

Markham, Ian S. *Engaging with Bediuzzaman Said Nursi: A Model of Interfaith Dialogue*. Farnham, England, and Burlington, VT: Ashgate, 2009.

Marshall, David, and Lucinda Mosher, eds. *Prayer: Christian and Muslim Perspectives. A Record of the Tenth Building Bridges Seminar, Convened by the Archbishop of Canterbury, Georgetown University School of Foreign Service in Qatar, 17–19 May 2011*. Washington, DC: Georgetown University Press, 2013.

Shenk, David W. *Christian, Muslim, Friend: Twelve Paths to Real Relationship*. Harrisonburg, VA: Herald Press, 2014.

Sudworth, Richard. *Distinctly Welcoming*. Queensway, England: Scripture Union, 2007.

Sudworth, Richard, with Andrew Smith and Gill Marchant. *Faith Values: Eight Complete Sessions on the Bible, Us, and Other Faiths*. Warwick, England: CPAS, 2007. www.cpas.org.uk/download/1190/FAITH_VALUES_ALL_LORES.pdf.

Troll, Christian W. *Muslims Ask, Christians Answer*. Hyde Park, NY: New City Press, 2012.

Volf, Miroslav, Ghazi bin Muhammad, and Melissa Yarrington, eds. *A Common Word: Muslims and Christians on Loving God and Neighbor*. Grand Rapids: Eerdmans, 2010.

Ward, Frances, and Sarah Coakley, eds. *Fear and Friendship: Anglicans Engaging with Islam*. London: Continuum, 2012.

Wright, Timothy. *No Peace without Prayer: Encouraging Muslims and Christians to Pray Together. A Benedictine Approach*. Monastic Interreligious Dialogue Series. Collegeville, MN: Liturgical Press, 2013.

Online

The Center for Anglican Communion Studies, Virginia Theological Seminary. www.vts.edu/anglican.

The Center for Anglican Communion Studies, Virginia Theological Seminary. www.youtube.com/watch?v=2gZeCsKLqbI.

A Common Word Between Us and You. www.acommonword.com.

Daughters of Abraham. www.daughtersofabraham.com.

Harvard University's Pluralism Project. pluralism.org.

Mahabba Network. mahabbanetwork.com.

Muslims Ask, Christians Answer. aam.s1205.t3isp.de/?L=1.

Muslimchristiandialogue.org. Muslim Christian Dialogue. www.muslimchristiandialogue.org.

Presence and Engagement. www.presenceandengagement.org.uk.

UK *Christian-Muslim Forum.* www.christianmuslimforum.org.

ABOUT THE AUTHORS

Munira Salim Abdalla was born on the island of Mombasa, Kenya, in East Africa. Her parents were the original Bantus and of Omani Arab descent. As a Muslim, she felt blessed to have parents give her the opportunity to attend a Catholic elementary school, a public secondary and high school, and the Seventh-day Adventist University of Eastern Africa in Kenya, which is affiliated with Andrews University in Michigan. In 1988, after moving to the United States, she worked as a professional fund-raiser and also as a regional advertising sales executive. She now serves on the boards of the Fredericksburg Area Food Bank, Rappahannock Community Health Center, and the Interfaith Council. Currently she is the executive director of Imani Multicultural Center and interfaith chaplain and chief administrator of Islamic Ummah of Fredericksburg, a new Islamic center in Fredericksburg, Virginia.

M. Imad Damaj, was born in Beirut, Lebanon, and attended college at the University of Paris, where he earned his doctorate in pharmacology in 1991. He is currently Professor of Pharmacology and Toxicology at Virginia Commonwealth University School of Medicine. Imad is faculty advisor for the Muslim Student Association at Virginia Commonwealth University. He is also the founder and president of the Virginia Muslim Coalition for Public Affairs. He is active in civic affairs in central Virginia.

David T. Gortner is director of the Doctor of Ministry Program and Professor of Evangelism and Congregational Leadership at Virginia Theological Seminary. He is an Episcopal priest with a Ph.D. in psychology and human development from the University of Chicago. David has served in educational, congregational, health-care, and public-ministry settings for more than twenty years. As a Christian leader, he has dedicated much of his ministry to strengthening clergy's religious leadership; empowering congregations in their faith, public witness, and community engagement; and building bridges between religious and secular organizations for the sake of healthier cities and neighborhoods. He taught and worked with Eboo Patel when he was first launching the Interfaith Youth Core, learned with great teachers about Islam, Buddhism, and the art of multi-faith education, and has continued to find ways to bring people of different faiths together for deep dialogue and meaningful community service.

Taalibah Hassan was born and raised in Washington, DC. She attended parochial schools in her early years and was exposed to and reclaimed Islam as her way of life while attending Boston University. She graduated from Howard University with both undergraduate and graduate degrees in education and taught advanced-placement biology and other science courses for more than thirty years. Taalibah has been involved with the Interfaith Conference of Metropolitan Washington for more than fifteen years, mainly as a passive participant in the annual concerts, until receiving facilitator training that ignited a passion for interfaith dialogue. She now is a practicing facilitator and is actively involved in interfaith activities several times a month.

She holds a graduate certificate in Muslim-Christian studies from the Washington Theological Consortium.

Claire Haymes served as program coordinator in the Center for Anglican Communion Studies at Virginia Theological Seminary from 2013 to 2016. Holding degrees from the University of Oxford and the University of Bath, she previously worked as staff interpreter and translator for the German federal government in the area of international development, subsequently interpreting and translating as a freelancer based variously in Washington, DC; Athens, Greece; and Bangkok. Claire has worshiped at Anglican churches in Europe, Africa, and Asia and has been active in three different churches in Northern Virginia. She is convinced of the transformative power of relationship-building and feels privileged to have worked in contexts where the relationships among people of faith, as they seek to be a part of the mission of God, are assigned such great importance.

Robert S. Heaney is an Anglican priest ordained in the Church of Ireland and is the director of the Center for Anglican Communion Studies and Associate Professor of Christian Mission, Virginia Theological Seminary. He holds doctorates in philosophical theology (Milltown Institute of Theology and Philosophy) and postcolonial theology (University of Oxford). Robert is the author of numerous articles and the book *From Historical to Critical Post-colonial Theology* (Pickwick, 2015).

Gay M. Rahn was one of the first women to be ordained to the diaconate in the Episcopal Diocese of Georgia in 1988 and ordained as priest in the Episcopal Diocese of Atlanta in 2000. She has served churches in Georgia, Tennessee, Florida, Massachusetts, and Virginia. Gay is currently serving as associate rector at St. George's Episcopal in Fredericksburg, Virginia, where she continues her work with children, youth and adult Christian formation and education, and world mission and interfaith relations. In addition to her service to the church and community, she also is a beekeeper.

William L. Sachs is an Episcopal priest and historian and the director of the Center for Interfaith Reconciliation at St. Stephen's Church in Richmond, Virginia. He is the author of six books and more than two hundred articles and reviews, most focused on modern Christianity's social experience. William was born in Richmond and earned his Ph.D. at the University of Chicago in the history of Christianity, after completing theological degrees at Vanderbilt and Yale. He has traveled across the Muslim world and has participated in interfaith conferences in the United States and abroad and served churches in Virginia, Connecticut, and Chicago.

Salih Sayilgan is a Ph.D. candidate in religion and culture in the School of Theology and Religious Studies at the Catholic University of America, where he also teaches courses on Islam, the Qur'an, and world religions. He received his M.A. in religious studies from the University of Alberta in Canada. Salih was first drawn to the interfaith enterprise through his work at a nongovernmental organization in Istanbul, where he had the opportunity to engage with scholars and activists from around the world. By listening to Christian theologians, he became interested in studying theology from a comparative perspective. He decided to spend a year as the first Muslim exchange student at Virginia Theological Seminary. It was at VTS where he had the chance to deepen his understanding of the Christian faith and also to meet many other faith practitioners in the diverse northern Virginia region.

Zeyneb Sayilgan grew up in Germany as the child of Kurdish Muslim immigrants from Turkey. She is the Senior Fellow in Peace and Reconciliation and the Henry Luce Muslim Visiting Professor at the Center for Anglican Communion Studies, Virginia Theological Seminary. Zeyneb holds a Ph.D. in theology from Georgetown University and is the book-review editor of the *Journal of Studies of Interreligious Dialogue* and a reviewer for the *Journal of Ecumenical Studies*.

Brandon E. Turner is a Ph.D. candidate in religion and culture at the Catholic University of America, where he is working on an ethnographic dissertation exploring how young American Muslims understand and/or define the notion of "being religious" in the American context. Within his home tradition of Christianity, his passion has most frequently been displayed in his attempts to bridge the "ecumenical gap" that exists between denominations. Within the larger context of world citizenship, he has worked to create dialogue between representatives of different faiths. His interests in interfaith work are rooted in the simple conviction that we all will benefit (academically *and* spiritually) when we take time to learn about other traditions and when we seek opportunities to befriend individuals who are different than us.

Hartley Wensing is the special projects coordinator in the Center for Anglican Communion Studies. She received her bachelor's degree in religion from Princeton University and her M.S. in educational policy studies at Florida State University. Her background includes extensive experience in cross-cultural programming and leadership development for youth and community engagement efforts in the United States and abroad. Her focus has included marginalized individuals and groups in Latin America, Asia, and the United States. She found that spiritual traditions and values were often the spark or sustenance in community-improvement efforts but that secular institutions mostly did not allow space for exploring these aspects. Hartley was raised and currently worships in the Episcopal Church, and she has found additional inspiration through her work and life experiences in Central America, Asia, and Native American communities.

Katherine Wood is a consultant and board member for nonprofit organizations following three decades of leadership experience in international diplomacy, higher education, and the arts in Washington, DC. She has a bachelor's degree in history from St. Olaf College, a Master of Music degree in flute performance from Boston University, and a Master of Divinity degree from Harvard Divinity School. From an early age she was interested in other countries and cultures and in what different artistic and religious forms of expression say about various ways of being human. Her faith journey has taken her to surprising and enriching places. Baptized a Methodist, she attended a Lutheran college, where she participated in Quaker meetings during the Vietnam War. Later she was drawn to Eastern contemplative practices while worshiping at an Anglo-Catholic parish that drew her into the Episcopal Church.